SHALOM
God's Masterplan

SHALOM
God's Masterplan

Steve Maltz

Saffron Planet
PO Box 2215
Ilford IG1 9TR
UK
T: +44 (0) 208 551 1719
E: contact@saffronplanet.net

Copyright (c) 2019 Steve Maltz

First published 2019

The right of Steve Maltz to be identified as the Author of this Work has been asserted by him in accordance with the Copyright, Designs and Patents Act 1988.

All rights reserved. No part of this publication may be reproduced, stored in a retrieval system, or transmitted in any form or by any means, electronic, mechanical, photocopying, recording or otherwise, without the prior permission of the publisher or a licence permitting restricted copying. In the UK such licenses are issued by theCopyright Licensing Agency, 90 Tottenham Court Road, London W1P 9HE.

Unless otherwise stated, Scripture quotations are taken from the
HOLY BIBLE, NEW INTERNATIONAL VERSION.
Copyright (c) 1973, 1978, 1984 by International Bible Society.

KJV – King James Version. Crown copyright.

ISBN 978-0-9931910-9-1

Cover design by Phil Maltz

Contents

Preface
Introduction

PART ONE: Our need for Shalom
Chapter One: From Shalom to separation   15
Chapter Two: A return to Shalom?   21
Chapter Three: An obstacle to Shalom   25
Chapter Four: Shalom thwarted   35
Chapter Five: Re-education   43
Chapter Six: Shalom and Ra   51

PART TWO: The Shalom of Salvation
Chapter Seven: Deplorables?   57
Chapter Eight: The Shalom of Salvation   63

PART THREE: The Shalom of Unity
Chapter Nine: Finding ourselves   67
Chapter Ten: Finding our function   73
Chapter Eleven: Finding the Church   81
Chapter Twelve: Finding Shalom   89
Chapter Thirteen: The Shalom of Unity   99

PART FOUR: The Shalom of Oneness
Chapter Fourteen: Shabbat, shalom?   109
Chapter Fifteen: Passover or pass me by?   121
Chapter Sixteen: The Shalom of Oneness   127

Chapter Seventeen: Simcha	135
Chapter Eighteen: Chaim	145
Chapter Nineteen: Kadosh	153
Chapter Twenty: Chesed	163
Chapter Twenty One: Mishpocha	171
Chapter Twenty Two: Limmud	179
Chapter Twenty Three: Berakhot	187
Chapter Twenty Four:	
What did the Gentiles ever do for us?	193
Chapter Twenty Five: Finding Oneness	205

PART FIVE: The Shalom of shaloms

Chapter Twenty Six: It happened in Devon	215
Chapter Twenty Seven: The Shalom of shaloms	223

Preface

The story never ends and I'm convinced that this is a good thing. Ever since I stood on London Bridge and God ignited a spark in me to investigate what being Hebraic actually meant, I have been on a journey. This journey has been a gradual revealing of truths, perhaps lost for centuries to the mainstream Church, but probably very real to those who truly "live the Life" without being bogged down by the theology of it all. For the past ten years God has nudged me forwards, allowing me fresh glimpses into the mindset that governed the very first Church of Peter, Paul and James. Patience not being one of my defining features, if I had only known that it would take the researching and writing of ten books to get to where I am now, in 2018, still on a journey...

With *How the Church lost the Way*, the extent of the damage that Plato did to the Church became real to me, ditto the following year with Aristotle in *How the Church Lost the Truth*. In *To Life!* the centrality of the Book of James became evident, a book that Martin Luther dismissed as "the epistle of straw", resulting in a good starting point for *Being Hebraic*, that of "faith in God underpinning our wisdom, which compels us to perform our deeds". Realising the mainstream Church's reliance on operating through a Greek mindset, I then worked through twenty areas where damage has ensued with *The Bishop's New Clothes* (and the *Naked Bishop*, a cut down version for Kindle). I then embarked on my Old Testament trilogy, with *God's Signature* focussing on the very building blocks of the Hebraic mindset, the Hebrew language itself, *God's Blueprint* looking at the content and themes of the Hebrew Scriptures themselves and *God's Tapestry* applying Hebraic principles to the Church in terms of how one should view such hot potatoes as the Sabbath, the Festivals and the Torah. Then, finally, my Hebraic Church trilogy. The first book, *Hebraic Church* looked mainly at the theology of a Hebraic mindset, introducing the concept of form and function among much else. *Livin' the Life* investigated practical applications, in how to "Be Hebraic", while we are *Being Church*. A key motif was the imperative of honouring God, reflecting Jesus and interacting with the Holy Spirit. Simple stuff, but also quite profound, and mostly neglected. The third book was *Into the Lion's Den*, last year, which suggested that the true Hebraic mindset needs to be adopted by the Church as the only realistic way of countering the madness that has entered our society in the form of political correctness, the rise of 'victim groups' and associated nuisances. Which brings us to today ...

Why another book? This was the annual groan by many in local fellowships, who considered that while many 'have a book in us', those who have a bucketload of books in them should be viewed with suspicion (and pity)! Such is the lot of a writer, who is compelled to write because he believes it is his God given mandate in life and nothing else.

In this book, naturally I will be building on what has come earlier, perhaps more than I have done before. This time, in the search for *shalom*, I will be picking up on two themes, one that recurred in every book since the very beginning of the journey, the other that was first introduced three books ago. The first theme is a negative one, one that has had a profoundly damaging impact on not just the Church but on Western culture. The second theme is quite wonderful and, when fully understood by all of us (including me), will, I believe, give us a precious touch on what makes God tick. The first is a tactic by the devil to stop mankind from achieving its destiny and the second is a gift of God to empower mankind in achieving its destiny. But, remarkably, a *third* theme emerged as a result of writing a bulk of this book. This is not surprising to me as every book is a personal odyssey and a time of great learning. This theme is significant enough to provide the by-line for this book, God's masterplan, and provides a hint to the places we are going to visit and what we are going to find when we get there.

All will be revealed as my journey now hopefully becomes your journey …

Introduction

My cosy little world was severely disrupted yesterday. No, it wasn't the three hour drive while feeling rather weary. Neither was it the three aged parents we were looking after on a short break to Geriatria-by-the-sea. Neither was it the sudden downfall while I was ferrying luggage to chalets, while dealing with frantic room-swapping. No, it was this - the sudden removal of what has become for me, and possibly you too, an ever-present and indispensable personal hub, connecting me to the world through sight and sound. *My iPhone had died on me.* Absolute disaster, I felt bereaved. There is a Hebrew word for how I was feeling. The word is *ra*, and the mildest form of it is when chaos reigns and nothing seems right or makes sense. The stronger form of the word is applicable to a society descending into division and anarchy, where freedom is restricted and order and justice are in short supply. I, of course, just had a brief taster of the milder form, quite trivial in the grand scheme of things, but enough to realise how fine the margins are between order and chaos, in the world we live in. The stronger form acts as a valid but frightening description of our current society. More on this a little later.

There is a word that is the opposite of *ra*. That word is *shalom*. The go-to word for Christians trying to demonstrate their Hebrew 'cred'. The ubiquitous word for comings ("hello") and goings ("goodbye") for Israelis. The Hebrew word that is perhaps the most misunderstood in its fullest sense. At its most general sense it takes the meaning of *peace*, which is how the Hebrew word is translated in the vast majority of instances in the Old Testament. In the New Testament, the Greek equivalent word is *eirene*, also translated as "peace" in virtually every instance. The online Catholic dictionary defines it also as "peace" and so does, interestingly, the Jewish Encyclopaedia. Add to that the Urban Dictionary and more or less every dictionary out there. So it seems an open and shut case. Or is it ... ?

Digging deeper into the Hebrew mind, we find that shalom (and *eirene*) begins to open up and reveal its secrets. We find that a better translation of the word is completeness, wholeness, well-being and restoration. The various Hebrew concordances (Strongs, NAS, Brown-Driver-Briggs) all convey the primary understanding of *completeness*, although the translators usually prefer the more general term of *peace*. Perhaps the latter has more of a poetic feel to it, but it is always important to consider the context in which the word is used. There are some crucial passages that we will be investigating, when the word 'peace' just does not do justice to the situation being described.

It's a far bigger picture than we may have imagined and it is well worth digging deeper. In this book we are going to look at ourselves and our society and investigate two things; that which *brings completeness* and that which *works against us finding completeness*. By doing so we will find ourselves entering struggles, conflicts and truths at the very heart of our faith and our walk with God and I guarantee that this is a journey worth hitching a ride on, for all who are serious about the current state of the Church and where it could be going to next.

PART ONE
Our need for Shalom

From Shalom to separation 1

The one who comes from heaven is above all. He testifies to what he has seen and heard, but no one accepts his testimony. Whoever has accepted it has certified that God is truthful. (John 3:31-33)

Here's our start point. *God is Truth*. This is as certain a statement that we can make, just like the related statement, *Man is not so truthful*. Our journey begins with this and we shall go right to the beginning to watch our story unfold.

Now for one of the saddest verses in the whole of the Bible.

Then the man and his wife heard the sound of the LORD God as he was walking in the garden in the cool of the day, and they hid from the LORD God among the trees of the garden. (Genesis 3:8)

We start off, I believe, with perfect **shalom**; completeness, wholeness and well-being. Think about it. Adam and Eve were used to their daily meetings *with God Himself* in the cool of the day. You really don't know how well off you are until you lose something special. And they had just lost *big time*. Something had happened to disrupt their shalom, to separate them from their Creator and their lives (and ours too) were never going to be the same.

They had eaten from the tree of the Knowledge of Good and Evil and their minds were now open to new possibilities, a new awareness (they now realised that they were naked, something that wasn't an issue before) and a new impulse, an insatiable search for knowledge, the aftertaste from the forbidden fruit. They had traded in their perfect fellowship with God for a life of search and discovery. They had moved from certainty – God is Truth – to the uncertainty of a life alone. No wonder they were full of shame and hid from God in the garden.

They had moved from *shalom*, wholeness, to *badal*, separation, from face-to-face chats with their Creator to a life of exclusion from the garden and of painful work and childbirth. This was the primary result of The Fall and it is going to reverberate through the halls of history. Cain kills his brother, Abel, and his punishment is further *separation*, banished to the land of Nod. Mankind at Babel built the tower in order to invade God's territory and 'to make a name for themselves'. God confounds their plans, confuses their language and *separates* them from each other, scattering them throughout the earth.

As the Hebrew Scriptures unfold, separation seems to be a divine principle, continuous movement, Abram and his family from Ur to Haran to Canaan, his cousin Lot separating off from the main party, Abraham's sons later migrating to other lands.

Of course, these separations were of a geographical nature and were little more than nudges from a loving God to spread mankind out in order to feed on natural resources that were also spread out. The true effects of the Fall in terms of *spiritual separation*, that between man and God, kick in after Moses has led the Hebrew slaves out of Egypt to the foot of Mount Sinai.

For you are a people holy to the LORD your God. The LORD your God has chosen you out of all the peoples on the face of the earth to be his people, his treasured possession. The LORD did not set his affection on you and choose you because you were more numerous than other peoples, for you were the fewest of all peoples. But it was because the LORD loved you and kept the oath he swore to your ancestors that he brought you out with a mighty hand and redeemed you from the land of slavery, from the power of Pharaoh king of Egypt. (Deuteronomy 7:6-8)

So, first God separates for Himself a people He could hopefully do business with. Here's a reminder, a bit further along in their journey:

For you singled them out from all the nations of the world to be your own inheritance, just as you declared through your servant Moses when you, Sovereign LORD, brought our ancestors out of Egypt. (1 Kings 8:53)

So mankind, from Adam and Eve separated from God in Eden, to a huge city of people, divided at Babel, is now divided again and God creates a nation, comprising of the Hebrew ex-slaves, to be His people, His representatives, His Kingdom of Priests, the *chosen* people.

But the separation does not end there.

The LORD also said to Moses, "I have taken the Levites from among the Israelites in place of the first male offspring of every Israelite woman. The Levites are mine, for all the firstborn are mine. When I struck down all the firstborn in Egypt, I set apart for myself every firstborn in Israel, whether human or animal. They are to be mine. I am the LORD." (Numbers 3:11-13)

Here are the *chosen* from the chosen, the Levites, the tribe of Israel that are to become the priests, God's *representatives* among His representatives. This is the system that was going to function for the people of Israel until the day came for it to be superseded by a better system.

Jesus has become the guarantor of a better covenant. Now there have been many of those priests, since death prevented them from continuing in office; but because Jesus lives forever, he has a permanent priesthood. Therefore he is able to save completely those who come to God through him, because he always lives to intercede for them. Such a high priest truly meets our need—one who is holy, blameless, pure, set apart from sinners, exalted above the heavens. Unlike the other high priests, he does not need to offer sacrifices day after day, first for his own sins, and then for the sins of the people. He sacrificed for their sins once for all when he offered himself. For the law appoints as high priests men in all their weakness; but the oath, which came after the law, appointed the Son, who has been made perfect forever. (Hebrews 7:22-28)

So, from Adam to Jesus, mankind has moved from *shalom*, completeness, to separation, from Adam and Eve enjoying direct fellowship with their Maker to the People of Israel, God's representatives separated from Him, with only the High Priest, taken from the tribe of the Levites, able to deal with Him on behalf of the people and even then just once a year.

He is to put on the sacred linen garments and make atonement for the Most Holy Place, for the tent of meeting and the altar, and for the priests and all the members of the community. "This is to be a lasting ordinance for you: Atonement is to be made once a year for all the sins of the Israelites." (Leviticus 16:32-34)

Just as the people of the world were split between the nations (*Goyim*) and His people, Israel, the people of Israel were themselves split between His tribe ('The Levites are mine') and the rest. This is Basic Old Testament theology 101. But it doesn't end there, as God has other systems in place. His Levitical priests may be there to serve Him, but He uses others to speak to and communicate His Word to His people. These are the *prophets*, from Abel to Zechariah, taken from all tribes or even no tribe (in pre-Exodus days).

Here are a group of people with thankless tasks, but only in terms of the *intended recipients* of the messages. Jesus reminds his generation about this:

Therefore this generation will be held responsible for the blood of all the prophets that has been shed since the beginning of the world, from the blood of Abel to the blood of Zechariah, who was killed between the altar and the sanctuary. (Luke 11:50-51)

Of course, not every prophet had an untimely end, but most had a hard time getting their message across to a people not always willing to listen. Nevertheless, they were all *acknowledged* as prophets.

Then there were the *Kings*. A sorry bunch apart from the odd shining light, but not even those luminaries were free from the occasional patch of darkness, witness Saul and his headstrong foolishness, or David and his adultery, or Solomon and his flesh-enticed idolatry, or any number of Kings of Judah and Israel, seduced by pagan promises. Kings, such as David, sometimes had a healthy relationship with God but they received their instructions, mostly in the form of admonishments, at the hands of the Prophet of that age.

So we can expand on our earlier analysis of the People of God. We still have two classes, those through whom God communicates and those He doesn't. The first group, the 'spiritual' ones, are comprised of prophets, priests and kings, and the rest are the 'physical' ones, the great body of the People of Israel.

This was, of course, all to change, when Jesus was crucified ... but did it?

A return to Shalom?

2

When Jesus came and died for us something amazing happened.

And when Jesus had cried out again in a loud voice, he gave up his spirit. At that moment the curtain of the temple was torn in two from top to bottom. (Matthew 27:50-51)

This was not just high drama, an incidental report to provide colour and intrigue to the momentous event unfolding just to the east of the Temple. It was also hugely significant.

In its first room were the lampstand and the table with its consecrated bread; this was called the Holy Place. Behind the second curtain was a room called the Most Holy Place, which had the golden altar of incense and the gold-covered ark of the covenant. This ark contained the gold jar of manna, Aaron's staff that had budded, and the stone tablets of the covenant. Above the ark were the cherubim of the Glory, overshadowing the atonement cover. (Hebrews 9:2-5)

This was the arrangement in the tabernacle in the wilderness and the temple in Jerusalem (though the ark had long gone) ... right up to the moment of Jesus' crucifixion. Then the curtain separating the Most Holy Place from the Holy Place was torn in two and *everything changed in a moment*. No longer was the High Priest to enter the Most Holy Place once a year on the Day of Atonement ... *to make atonement in the Most Holy Place until he comes out, having made atonement for himself, his household and the whole community of Israel.* (Leviticus 16:17)

The curtain was no more, now *all* potentially have

access to the Most Holy Place, through Jesus' death on the cross. All that is required is sufficient faith to embrace this awesome truth. We slip from the restrictions of Isaiah 59:2:

But your iniquities have separated you from your God; your sins have hidden his face from you, so that he will not hear.

… to the new glorious realities of Hebrews 10:19-22:

Therefore, brothers and sisters, since we have confidence to enter the Most Holy Place by the blood of Jesus, by a new and living way opened for us through the curtain, that is, his body, and since we have a great priest over the house of God, let us draw near to God with a sincere heart and with the full assurance that faith brings, having our hearts sprinkled to cleanse us from a guilty conscience and having our bodies washed with pure water.

From a separation between man and his Maker that has lasted since the days of Adam, to the possibilities of true *shalom* and completeness, the shalom of salvation. The way has been opened. Surely the world would now change because who could resist this free gift? Who wouldn't want to be able to draw near to God, without needing a High Priest in any way? If only things were that simple.

There is another shalom now made possible through this momentous act. Not only could we now be reconciled to God, but also to each other, in a shared community of believers, connected by this shared faith in all that Jesus has done for us.

Just as a body, though one, has many parts, but all its many parts form one body, so it is with Christ. For we were all baptized by one Spirit so as to form one body – whether Jews or Gentiles, slave or free – and we were all given the one Spirit to drink. Even so the body is not made up of one part but of many. (1 Corinthians 12:12-14)

How wonderful is this? Not only are we guaranteed

access to God, but now we have an invisible spiritual connection to all who share the same Spirit, from separation to a shalom of unity. What a mighty army we now are, what great things we can achieve together! What can stop us now?

But there's more. God has even made provisions for reconciliation between those with *prior form*, who have already been members of God's covenant people for centuries, and those with no history at all, who are grafted in from outside, strangers to the ways of God. Jews and Gentiles were now to live and work together, in mutual respect of each other, without prejudice. We read this in Ephesians 2, from verse 11 onwards:

Therefore, remember that formerly you who are Gentiles by birth and called "uncircumcised" by those who call themselves "the circumcision" (which is done in the body by human hands)– remember that at that time you were separate from Christ, excluded from citizenship in Israel and foreigners to the covenants of the promise, without hope and without God in the world. But now in Christ Jesus you who once were far away have been brought near by the blood of Christ.

So here Paul first offers assurances to the Gentiles, *foreigners to the covenants of the promise*. Let's read the rest of the passage slowly and deliberately.

For he himself is our peace ...

Jesus is the **shalom**, the one who is going to bring completeness. He is the one who is going to make the necessary provisions.

... who has made the two groups one and has destroyed the barrier, the dividing wall of hostility, by setting aside in his flesh the law with its commands and regulations.

He has provided a better way ('a better covenant' Hebrews 8:6) by providing equal access to God for both Jew and Gentile, just *one way to salvation.*

His purpose was to create in himself one new humanity out of the two thus making peace ...

Or 'one new man' to be less P.C., an expression of the shalom of oneness.

... and in one body to reconcile both of them to God through the cross, by which he put to death their hostility. He came and preached peace to you who were far away and peace to those who were near. For through him we both have access to the Father by one Spirit.

Both Jew and Gentile equally meet Jesus at the cross and have access to God through the Holy Spirit.

So, to summarise, we have the shalom of salvation, whereby everyone has a chance of reconciliation with God, the shalom of unity, whereby all reconciled believers have a place and a function in His Kingdom and finally the shalom of oneness, with Jews and Gentiles fully reconciled and equal under God.

This is how it is meant to be. This is God's intended shalom for us, completeness in relationships between man and God and between believers in Jesus. It *could* have been so good.

The fact that this has never fully happened is not a flaw in the plan, *but a flaw in our execution of God's perfect plan.* Why would this be so? The story now begins to unravel ...

An obstacle to Shalom

3

About the time that Malachi, the last Old Testament prophet, gave his final prophecy, things were stirring around eight hundred miles to the west. It was the 4th Century BC and a small country was busy churning out a never-ending collection of amazingly clever people. Socrates was the key man at this time. A pug-ugly little man in flowing robes, he was incredibly influential then and now, yet wrote nothing down. That was left to Plato, his pupil.

Taller, younger and more dignified, he cast his teacher as the chief character in a series of dialogues with others. He explains:

Before my learned teacher entered the scene, we philosophers concerned ourselves with the world around us. Is the world made up of earth, air, fire and water, or are there smaller building blocks? Does mathematics govern everything? What about poetry? Socrates changed all that. What he taught us is to look within, at our moral beings, at what makes us tick ...

Socrates was indeed influential, even for modern day thinkers. So key was he that all who preceded him were lumped together in a single classification, the "Presocratics", the string of warm up acts, preparing the audience for the main performer. Socrates was a familiar figure in the streets of Athens. He was an effective teacher, his classrooms mainly the public spaces, his pupils taken from the rich young men of his day, with time on their hands and rebellion in their hearts. He taught them logic and the ability to reason. On the positive side, one effect of this teaching was the jettisoning of the sorry, pathetic and argumentative bunch of Greek gods that had held sway for so long. Not so positive for him was that he was condemned to death by a repressive city government for 'corrupting the young' and, most tellingly, 'neglecting the gods'.

Plato was Socrates' disciple. He was his biographer and recorded his ideas and became, in his own right, perhaps the most influential of all Socrates' pupils. He founded a school in Akademia, a suburb of Athens, the very first "academy". There people were instructed in mathematics, geometry, law and the natural sciences, as well as philosophy. He also wrote much. Many of his early writings were expanding on the ideas of Socrates, who now comes under the spotlight.

There's a theory regarding Socrates, that he drew much from the rabbis of his day. One clue is in the similarity between their ways of teaching; the *Socratic method* is the way that he teased the truth out of his students through the continued asking of questions, often exposing a fallacy or contradiction in the initial argument, but arriving at a conclusion together, which is more satisfying than the listen-to-the-lecturer-and-shut-up-approach to learning! This is the same approach used often by Jesus himself, for instance, when he was quizzed on a matter of authority in Matthew 21:23-27:

Jesus entered the temple courts, and, while he was teaching, the chief priests and the elders of the people came to him. "By what authority are you doing these things?" they asked. "And who gave you this authority?" Jesus replied, "I will also ask you one question. If you answer me, I will tell you by what authority I am doing these things. John's baptism—where did it come from? Was it from heaven, or of human origin?" They discussed it among themselves and said, "If we say, 'From heaven,' he will ask, 'Then why didn't you believe him?' But if we say, 'Of human origin'– we are afraid of the people, for they all hold that John was a prophet." So they answered Jesus, "We don't know." Then he said, "Neither will I tell you by what authority I am doing these things.

The question to ask is whether Jesus was using the Socratic method or whether Socrates was using the Jesus method or, to be more specific, the *rabbinic method* that Jesus would have been trained to use when he was growing up. Personally, this is just a sideshow and a question that scholars have, as of yet, failed to fully answer, though there is an intriguing passage in the Jewish writings, the *Aggada,* where it is remarked that Socrates was a disciple of Ahithophel, one of Israel's greatest ever sages and a counsellor of King David. He was, unfortunately, also a bit of a rogue and managed to betray David, followed by a suicide, said to be a type of Judas Iscariot's similar behaviour. Seems rather a strange role model for Socrates to have, but legends can often be ancient expressions of Fake News, so we shouldn't take such episodes too seriously.

Nevertheless, there is the possibility of an intriguing link between the rabbis of the Old Testament and Socrates of ancient Greece and the reason I bring this up is suggested by the theme developed in the previous chapter. We were looking at the Hebrews' relationship with God in Old Testament times and arrived at two classes, those through whom God communicates and those He doesn't. The first group, the 'spiritual' ones, comprise prophets, priests and kings, and the rest are the 'physical' ones, the great body of the People of Israel. Hold on to that thought as we return to Socrates.

Plato, the pupil of Socrates, as I've remarked in earlier books, had ideas that were to become almost as influential as Jesus in the development of Western Christianity. And many of these ideas came from Socrates, including perhaps his greatest (and most damaging) contribution to the world of philosophy, *The Theory of Forms*.

Plato and Socrates were men of ideas, but thought little of the world that surrounded them. Plato wrote about two worlds, the obvious one that we live in and a "perfect" one, *somewhere else in the Universe*. I suppose this would be his concept of heaven and in this heaven exists what Plato called *Forms*.

To understand what these are, we need to think about everything that we see around us in our world, from actual objects like chairs and diamonds, to geometric shapes like squares and triangles, to concepts like beauty and goodness. Now you must realise that, according to Plato, all of these things are just imperfect copies of perfect chairs, diamonds, squares, triangles, beauty and goodness, that exist in the other "perfect" world. These items of perfection are Plato's *Forms*. Get your (imperfect) head around that, then!

Plato also believed that whereas most of us will never get to see these Forms, some of us would. These are the *guardians*, specially gifted and trained individuals, the philosophers of course! Plato explained all of this in his analogy of the cave.

Our lives are as prisoners deep inside a cave, where all we can see of objects are their shadows, projected on the wall by a fire. We believe that what we see is reality but we are mistaken. To see reality we have to leave the cave and see things as they really are, though most are content at just seeing the shadow shapes inside the cave.

According to Plato, the one who makes this step to leave the cave is the *guardian*, who is rewarded by viewing the "higher Good", the source of all truth and reason. Here, perhaps, is a link to the Old Testament scenario of priests, prophets and kings, though there is a major difference between these *kosher* guardians and the ones Plato had in mind. For him, the "higher Good" is the ultimate Form, Plato's concept of God, though not the personal God as we know Him. This "higher Good" is what we must aspire to. This "higher Good" is an eternal reality that exists in a higher realm and our physical senses are just not equipped enough to see any more than a pale reflection. Plato likens this concept to the sun in two ways. Both cause things to exist and grow and both are sources of light. As it is light which enables our eyes to have a partial sight of reality, then "the higher Good" enables our minds to have partial knowledge of what is real. So there is space for the concept of God, albeit an *impersonal* one, in Plato's philosophy. Plato's God does not answer prayers, or comfort those in distress, or teach his people or listen to the cries of the heart. Plato's God is most assuredly not our Father in Heaven. So Plato may have got the idea from Socrates, who may have got the idea from the rabbis, but *it certainly wasn't God they were referring to in their new philosophy.*

But it goes further and this is where the real damage comes from. Plato believed that there are absolute standards for such things as goodness, morality and truth, each of these existing as a perfect Form in this "second" world. He also believed in the eternal soul and that we are body and soul. He thought that these were totally separate entities, bound together temporarily during a person's lifetime. This was the concept of the duality of man. But, to Plato, the soul was the dominant, superior entity and it is immortal, being reborn again and again in different bodies, gaining in knowledge as it does so, like the concept of re-incarnation in Eastern religions. The soul is our seat of thought and knowledge, associated with the "second" perfect world. The body interacts through the five senses with our *imperfect* world and, to Plato, restricts the soul from attaining its full potential. So, in his view, the soul is good and the body is bad. **Everything associated with the soul is good, everything associated with the body is bad.** This is his big idea and around it much of history revolved.

Thanks to the Gentile Church Fathers, *dualism* invaded the early Church once the original Jewish leadership had died out, taking away with them the Hebraic mindset of Jesus and all who preceded him. It was time for the pagans to run the show and although they were professed 'new creations' in Christ, there was enough of the old to ensure an unhealthy mix and, prominent among this was the effect of the dualism of *Platonism*, which had now become perhaps the dominant philosophy in the Roman world of the early Church. Here is an idea of the damage this did, summarised from my earlier book, *How the Church lost The Way*.

We can start at the Creation story. To Plato, the Universe came into being through the work of the *Demiurge*, not quite God as we know Him, but a lesser god. Dualism implies that anything of the physical world is *inferior* to anything of the spiritual world. So this Demiurge, responsible for the Creation of the physical Universe, just has to be an inferior god, from Plato's point of view. Marcion, a heretic from the First Century, took this further and divided the whole Bible up according to dualism. For him the God (Demiurge), the people (the Jews) and the scripture of the Old Testament are physical and therefore *inferior*, whereas the God (Jesus), the people (Christians) and the scripture of the New Testament are spiritual and therefore *superior*. This notion fed into the "Christian" anti-Semitism, masquerading as 'replacement theology' or supercessionism that still reigns in some parts of the Church and is nothing more than pandering to a pagan alien mindset, as well as hatred that may lurk in the deepest part of the soul.

When Plato says that the soul is good and the body is bad, he is declaring a basic principle that has many guises. In religious terms, he is saying that the physical world, the one in which we live, is bad (or evil) and the spiritual world (heaven and such places) is good, and therefore worth striving for. So, material world is bad ... spiritual world is good. This theme is going to pop up again and again in Christian thought and practice, as you begin to realise how deep this idea has sunk into our collective minds.

Because of this, many of the gentile Church Fathers were uncomfortable whenever, in the Bible, God (a spiritual being) mixes it with us on a human level (the material world), when He interacts with man personally, or shows human characteristics or emotions. When they considered such God-man interactions they would look beyond any literal interpretations of the verse for deeper meanings, *allegories*, often looking for deeper "spiritual" meanings behind Bible verses that the author (God) meant just to be taken literally.

A favourite theme would be to re-interpret the Old Testament in the light of the New Testament, using techniques from Greek philosophy, married with insights from early Christian tradition and other writings. The driving principle was that the Bible contained three levels of meaning, corresponding to the body, soul and spirit. You can see the influence of Plato here, particularly when they consider that the "body" level of meaning, the literal meaning of the text, is for the more simple minded whereas the "soul" and more particularly the "spirit" levels of meaning are for the *more enlightened* readers. The scene has now been firmly established that, because of the demands of the Platonic world view in preferring the spiritual over the material, spiritual meanings were sought, even in Bible passages that were so obviously meant to be taken literally. A free-for-all was now created, allowing Christian teachers right up to the current day to be able to bend and coax God's Word to say whatever they want it to say!

It may have been just one tiny idea, but it produced some major effects. With Greek philosophy so embedded in Christian thought it is now possible to see how heresies begin. We have already seen Marcionism, from the heresy of Marcion in dividing up the Old and New testament in opposition to each other. Then there was Jesus himself. Another heresy called *Docetism* declared that God was a spiritual being and couldn't take a physical form. So Jesus couldn't possibly have had a real body, he just *seemed* to have one. He was therefore an illusion, as was the crucifixion! You can see how this dualist approach would have confused them. We know Jesus as fully God and fully man, but to these people, educated to believe that only "spiritual" is good, how can Jesus be expressed also in the "physical"? They just couldn't get their heads around it!

In fact heresies abounded in the first few centuries of the Christian era. Here are a few more. *Apollinarianism* stated that Jesus had a human body, a lower soul and a divine mind. *Eutychianism* suggested that Jesus' human nature was overcome by the divine nature. *Montanism* exercised a sort of extreme Pentecostalism. *Monarchianism* insisted that God was a single person. *Nestorianism* argued that Christ existed as two persons.

Sabellianism declared that everything was how the

believer perceived it to be, whatever that was meant to mean! They were either named after the person who thought them up or after the Greek word for the principal idea.

It is surely plain to see that this was the natural outcome of viewing Christianity as a philosophy rather than a pure faith. While Christian philosophers were debating Platonic principles applied to the Father, Son and Holy Spirit, their followers were killing each other in the name of the Father, Son and Holy Spirit (and Plato).

Shalom thwarted   4

We are now going to see how Greek thinking has wormed its way into the very fabric of our Christian life. Virtually every Christian reference book, when speaking of influences during the formative years of the Church, agrees and accepts that Greek philosophical ideas were key to the understanding of the fundamental doctrines. No criticism or regret, just blithe acceptance, as if the pagan polluting of the faith in Jesus Christ is just one of those things, as if the Bible alone was not sufficient for our understanding of God and His dealings with mankind!

For a start, the immediate effect of declaring the body as bad and soul as good is an obvious one. If the body is bad then so are things associated with the body, particularly voluntary processes like sex. To the early Church, those who followed "spiritual" careers, in the Church, were expected to be celibate, a practice that still continues in the modern day Catholic Church and which has indirectly cost the Vatican millions of dollars in compensation claims (figure that one out for yourself). A Catholic view is still that celibacy is a "higher calling", in the sense of remaining pure until heaven beckons, when you will be united with Christ directly. Then there were the flagellants and their like, who believed that only by scourging or whipping themselves could they achieve favour with God. They tended to appear during the plague seasons, such as during the Black Death in Europe, when they marched through the lands, whipping and beating themselves, in a misplaced idea of atoning for the sins of the world and appeasing an "angry" God. So the ideas of Plato had convinced the Church that anything associated with our physical bodies was bad. It devalues our lives on earth and fixes the idea in our minds that we should not place any worth in our earthly existence and yearn for heaven. You've heard the expression of *being so heavenly minded that you're no earthly good* and you can blame Plato's influence for this! It encourages us to see our faith just as a "ticket to heaven" rather than the service we are meant to give in this world, particularly in the context of the Great Commission. Of course, heaven is our great hope and reward, but that should not be at the expense of a fulfilled life, of service, sacrifice and testimony.

Here lies the real problem. Declaring a division between heaven and earth, between sacred work and secular work, between the holy and the profane, between clergy and laity, between the supernatural and the natural, is a thoroughly Greek idea, coming from this *dualism* of Plato. It leads to a separation between "spiritual" occupations and the rest and has given us an unconscious respect for those of us with a *higher calling*. It fuels such attitudes as believing that missionaries, church workers, clergy and those "called out for Christian service" are the only real full-time Christians there are. The rest of us, working in offices, schools, building sites and the like, are "part time" Christians, defined by what we do for God *away* from the workplace.

We are all priests, because we all have access to God through Jesus, by the power of the Holy Spirit. Yet many of us act as if this is not true, we still shove our pastors, teachers, preachers, worship leaders and even Christian celebrities onto pedestals and conference platforms and look to them to minister to us and show us Jesus. This is a thoroughly Greek idea and wrong! We don't need these people to "offer sacrifices" on our behalf, we are all priests and we can all approach Jesus directly. We don't need to venerate dead bones or those who have cast off their mortal coil in glorious triumph. Dead saints can't hear your prayers, only God can. We are all saints, even though we may not always act very saintly. We are no less special than anyone else who has gone before us. We are the Church, we are all priests and saints. We *all* have a higher calling. There is no sacred and secular, because we are all sacred, we all have a sacred calling.

If anyone destroys God's temple, God will destroy him; for God's temple is sacred, and you are that temple. (1 Corinthians 3:17)

Greek thinking tells us that the missionary, who travels overseas to work in a Christian village, showing God's love to those who haven't experienced it, is to be especially revered. Not to demean the sacrifice these people have made and the hardships they will undoubtedly endure, is this any different to those of you with a standard 9 to 5 job in an office, working in a thoroughly (and often aggressively) non-Christian environment, where any attempt at communicating your faith would be met with hostility, exclusion and even law suits? Who has the higher calling? Neither, because wherever we are in the world we are called to be witnesses.

All that God expects of us is to "be in the world but not of the world". We are to be salt and light in our witness to the world, without being sucked into its ways. Not easy and getting harder all the time! James reminds us of the consequences.

... don't you know that friendship with the world is hatred toward God? Anyone who chooses to be a friend of the world becomes an enemy of God. (James 4:4)

And speaking of work, we hear a lot of folk working to

live rather than living to work. Given the choice, most of us would prefer to work less and play more. Well that's a Greek idea too, devaluing the act of working for a living and encouraging us to look forwards to weekends, when the real living takes place! Let's party is the mantra of today, borne from the Greek lifestyle philosophy of hedonism. The Ancient Greeks were people of leisure, manual work was left to the slaves. For Jews it was a lot different – for some of their history they were the slaves - but that's not the point I wish to make. The pattern of their attitude was set in the second chapter of the Bible.

By the seventh day God had finished the work he had been doing; so on the seventh day he rested from all his work. (Genesis 2:2)

God wasn't afraid to roll His sleeves up and get on with it. He expected man to do the same.

The LORD God took the man and put him in the Garden of Eden to work it and take care of it. (Genesis 2:15)

There is great satisfaction in working, a sense of earning your keep and adding to the common good. It is also God's plan for us. He didn't create us to spend our lives in selfish pursuits; leisure time and entertainment should be a reward for our toil, not an end in itself. Unfortunately many in the Church today act as if it is. *Did you enjoy the worship today? No, not really, perhaps we should go to a livelier Church!*

Having attacked one or two sacred cows I may as well upset the whole herd now. There's nothing special about a church building. It's just a place where Christians hang out. It's no more or less sacred or holy than anywhere else. The altar is just a table for bread and wine. The act of Communion is holy but the elements of the process are just ordinary old bread and wine. These ideas are all from Greece, telling us that what we deem as "spiritual", even a building for meeting, is to be sought after. In fact God doesn't just float around waiting to be summoned by His flock into certain chosen acceptable places. God is everywhere, even in brothels, crack dens and the White House, just as Jesus never hesitated in visiting places that the religious elite wouldn't dream of setting foot in.

While Jesus was having dinner at Matthew's house, many tax collectors and "sinners" came and ate with him and his disciples. When the Pharisees saw this, they asked his disciples, "Why does your teacher eat with tax collectors and 'sinners'?" (Matthew 9:10-11)

The word *pastor* comes from the Latin word for "shepherd", referring to an individual who would care for his flock. Of course pastors perform this function, but they tend also to be the administrator, leader, teacher, preacher etc. etc. It is the Churches' equivalent to the secular CEO, the top of the heap, the head of the hierarchy, the man with the desk slogan, "the buck stops here". Before the pastor was established, the early Church had no titles or offices or complex hierarchies. Everything was done in an informal manner by the elders and apostles. Then in a process started by Ignatius of Antioch, in the First Century, a hierarchy slowly began to take shape within the Church, with the bishop taking on more and more responsibilities. He became the equivalent of today's pastor, as leader and spokesman, with his finger in every pie. The word *clergy,* referring to the people who did all the work in the Church, started to appear, as well as *laity,* referring to everyone else and the die was cast in separating "professional" Christians from the rest of us. Earlier there was a suggestion that this basic concept could have been borrowed partly from the rabbis, who drew a distinction between Old Testament *clergy* (priests, prophets and kings) and *laity* (the rest). Interesting – isn't the Church meant to be based on a *New Testament* model? What has Socrates done? What has the Church done?

So the Church developed hierarchies, great human edifices that served to distance the common man from his God. Christians were no longer a "priesthood of all believers" (1 Peter 2:9) and access to God was now controlled by the middle-men of the clergy, who controlled every aspect of life and became a privileged caste of society, even exempt from paying taxes or serving in the army.

Sunday, when most of us go to Church, is just a day of the week, incidentally named after the Sun god (the emperor Constantine called it *the venerable day of the Sun*, intending it to become the Christian day of worship). Are we just Sunday Christians? If we are then we are just closet Greeks. We are saying that our times for personal holiness are just that hour or two on Sunday morning and the rest of the week belongs to us. Those Church visiting times are not particularly special to God, what He wants from us is 24/7 reality, lives dedicated to worshipping and serving Him even at 7:30pm on a Monday when our favourite soap is on the box.

So you should now have a good grasp of the damage done by Plato's dualism in the Church. It's all about division and separation, clergy and laity, holy and profane, natural and supernatural and so on.

It's no wonder that the shalom that God intended for us as a result of Jesus' work on the cross, has been thwarted in so many ways. It has kept many away from fulfilling their potential within the Kingdom and has certainly ensured that the 'One New Man' ideal of Jew and Gentile in the Kingdom has never found true expression in all of the centuries of Gentile domination of the Church.

Remember back to the Preface, where we looked not just at *shalom* and its theme of completeness, but at its nemesis, *ra*, the polar opposite, representing chaos, anarchy and division. We have now seen, in this chapter, the playing out of *ra* in society and the Church, forcing back any hope of *shalom*. In fact, the very core principle of Platonism is to bring division and to keep any sense of completeness at bay.

So, how do we deal with this? The first response in acknowledging a historical problem surely is to ensure that it doesn't become a problem in the present and the future. In our search for true shalom in our Christian life it is now time for the fightback.

It starts here.

Re-education   5

It's a simple enough problem. God wants us to be complete and whole, whether it is you and I as individuals, or the Church as a complete worldwide and regional body. He wants us to find the shalom of salvation in our relationship with Him, the shalom of unity in our relationship with fellow believers and the shalom of oneness in the dynamic between Jew and Gentile. Realistically, the problems of the wider Body of Christ are not going to be solved within these pages, so you and I are going to do the only thing we are able to do and that is *do our best to get things right as individuals*. And only then can we hope and pray that we can influence others, in accordance with whatever function God has in store for us. This can be quite an exciting journey, I hope you have buckled up.

Platonism brought division, whether it is in how we worship, read the Bible, live our lives, allocate our resources, order our Church services and so on. By creating a wedge between the "physical" and "spiritual" and deeming the latter preferable to the former, it created artificial divisions between clergy and laity, supernatural and natural, holy and profane, sacred and secular. These divisions are embedded into the DNA of our Church life, whether we choose to accept this or not. It has created a Church that has mostly accepted a model developed by secular corporations; led from the front, hierarchical and non-collaborative. It has produced Christians who rarely impact their environment, outside the safety of their

Church bubbles. Along with other aspects of Greek thinking it has produced a 'man-centred' Christianity, suffused with the individualism, ambitions and naturalistic world-view of our godless secular society, rather than the 'God-centred' force of nature it was intended to be.

The solution is as obvious as it is difficult. We need to first accept that change is needed, then be open enough to be agents of change ourselves. This *change* is not a trivial matter, though, it is not a matter of taking a pill, reading a book or changing a few habits. It is an acknowledgement that the Church, in its formative years, has ingested some dodgy material that is still stuck in the system. Ideally we need a purge and a switch to a healthier diet, but that's not going to work in our case as we are dealing with a Church, as I said earlier, that has a DNA that has been modified. Jettisoning the tiresome metaphors, what this actually means is that the Greek mindset is thoroughly embedded in most aspects of the Western Church, in how it thinks and how it acts. It's not just the dualism of Plato, but it is also the reliance on the rational approach of Aristotle, as a counterpoint to the supernaturalism of a faith environment driven by the Hebraic mindset of Jesus and the Jews in Biblical times. In short, the Greek mindset does not provide the best tools for living a faith-filled life, where a belief in the 'miracle maker' is the defining feature. This is a good point for a brief primer into the differences between the Greek and Hebraic mindset, so you can appreciate the scale of the problem.

Firstly, a potted history of the mainstream Church in the West, to see the effects of Greek thinking. The following is taken from "Hebraic Church":

The established mainstream Church first left the rails

as soon as the original apostles had died, leaving the legacy of Jesus in the hands of Gentiles educated in the Greek-speaking world and immersed in the philosophic ideas of Ancient Greece, particularly the dualism of Plato, which separated the spiritual from the physical, with the former being preferred to the latter. Heresies, such as *Marcionism* and *Gnosticism*, abounded, borne out of corruptions of God's word through these ideas from Greek philosophy and these were countered through the efforts of early Church fathers such as Justin Martyr and Irenaeus, who, themselves were self-styled Christian philosophers. So the Christian world in those days was fought overby Greeks versus Greeks, with the only real casualty being the gospel itself.

It was in the ancient city of Alexandria when things really started to get worse, thanks firstly to the Church Father, Clement, who was by today's standard a heretic in all but name, and Origen, who did immeasurable damage in the area of Bible interpretation, popularising the use of *allegory* in his approach to Holy Scripture and opening up the floodgates for ages to come, allowing "teachers" to coax any meaning they liked out of their reading of the Bible.

Then came the Dark Ages, a period of ignorance, superstition and... darkness. Although the Bible was now available, few could actually read it, apart from the professional class of Christians, the clergy. Some of the blame for these sorry times could be laid at the feet of the foremost Christian teacher of that day, Augustine. He wrote a book, *City of God*, as a defence of Christianity against the paganism that surrounded it. In the book, he encouraged his readers, (in a Christian take on the dualism of Platonism,) to pay less attention to their lives and, instead, look heavenwards at the "city yet to come", the *City of God*, or Heaven. Hence the Dark Ages, when nobody really cared about anything apart from the promises of the after-life, were dictated by the State Church with its system of sacraments, rather than by the authentic route of repentance of sins and trust in the death and resurrection of Jesus Christ!

In the 8th Century the works of another Greek philosopher, Aristotle, were discovered by the Muslims and translated by the Jews into the languages of the day. By introducing the concept of *rationalism* into the religious cultures of the Jews, Muslims and Christians, it is fair to say that the damage done was immense. These ideas were taken up by the most influential Christian philosopher of the Middle Ages, Thomas Aquinas, who created a religious system combining faith and reason, stating that even the existence of God was not to be taken as a given but through analysis of information that could be gathered by the senses.

The genie had been let out of the bottle and the subsequent rise of rationalism was to eat away at the certainties of faith. State Christianity became more of a philosophic system to be argued over than a supernatural expression of God's plans for mankind. This was not helped by the corruptions of the Catholic Church and its use of pagan practices to control the ordinary people. Something had to give and it was Martin Luther who provided the spark of a *Reformation* in the Church, a new beginning.

Yet even the Reformers were not free from Greek influences, following the Platonism of Augustine in many of their ideas, as distinct from the Roman Catholics, who stuck to the Aristotelianism of Thomas Aquinas. It was the accent on the rationalism of Aristotle that was to spearhead the next major attack on the Christian Church, which has lasted from the end of the Middle Ages right up until today. First came the *Renaissance*, the "rebirth", the flowering of culture and artistic expression in Italy, believe it or not inspired by the ideals of Ancient Greece! This was also the birth of *Humanism*, a movement that placed man at the centre of everything, rather than God. Then came the philosophers of the *Enlightenment*, who built on these ideas and eventually did away totally with the need for God, replacing Him with their own rational ideas. This gave birth to *Individualism*, which has now become the defining feature of modern society.

Although God made something of a comeback thanks to the Methodist movement, followed by the awakenings of the 18th and 19th Centuries, prompting a massive worldwide missionary movement, we largely entered an age of confusion and division. This was the age of new cults, such as Christian Science and the Jehovah's Witnesses, borne out of the ancient Greek heresies. It was also an age of a fight back by the Catholics, with strange new doctrines such as the *Immaculate Conception*. There were the Deists, who believed in some kind of absentee landlord God and then there was Charles Darwin and his ideas, to further chip away at the ancient faith, with the mallet of human reason and scientific methodology. And out of Germany came *Higher Criticism*, a new way to disbelieve the Bible.

Which brings us to the modern age, where our story ends, though the problems don't, as we are still held bound by Greek thought. It hasn't gone away, it has just embedded itself into our thought processes. Deep surgery is needed, now that we have made the diagnosis. We need to start to think about a cure.

The cure is simply a return to the mindset of Jesus, the first apostles and the Jewish society in which they lived.

The following is taken from *"Livin' the Life"*:

Let's start with an initial working definition of what is *Hebraic*. The starting point is having a *faith* in God that underpins our *wisdom*, which compels us to perform our *deeds* (rather than thinking or debating or arguing about such things). This definition is gradually refined as God reveals more and more. It bucks the trend of current perceptions that define Hebraic in terms of *externals*, of practices, rituals and Jewish cultural trappings. Instead the true Hebraic understanding is of an *internal mindset*, that of Jesus and his disciples and in fact of the Jews who preceded him and inhabited the pages of the Hebrew Bible. In other words, rather than dwelling on festivals, eating habits and vocabulary, we consider how those early Jews *thought and acted on those thoughts*. Following on from that I contrasted Greek and Hebraic thinking and came to the following conclusions:

The first was that we should *live Hebraically*, focusing on our **relationships**. There should be reverence for God, a total respect and unquestioning faith in God in every situation. We should favour small groups, with an emphasis on personal relationships within the Church and nurture family relationships, with the realisation that God's blessings flow more freely through His covenant people.

The second was that we should *think Hebraically*, focusing on **understanding God's provisions for us**. We should consider living by faith, a total reliance on God's promises for our needs. We should have total trust in the Bible, treating God's Word as precious, completely timeless and truthful and endeavouring to study it wholeheartedly. We should also focus on the *real* Jesus, understanding him in his Jewish setting.

The third was that we should act *Hebraically*, living lives of truth, joy and purpose. There is the importance of good conduct, showing the world by our actions that there is something different about us. We should seek an understanding of the concept of One New Man and make adjustments if necessary. Then there is unity without compromise, supporting our Christian family without condoning error and heresy.

The Hebraic is about man and God and can be better understood through this set of contrasts.

- The Greek mind says that *man* is at the centre of life; the Hebraic mind says that *God* is at the centre of life.

- The Greek mind says that the things of God must be deduced from our logical minds; the Hebraic mind says that the things of God can only be understood by faith and revelation.

- The Greek mind says that we should strive for knowledge about God; the Hebraic mind says that we should *know* God.

It's all *Hebraic*. It's a lost art for some, to others it's already an ever-present reality. It's simply how we can best act out our part in the divine drama, the everlasting love story of God and His people. To do so we need to discover our role and purpose and see where we fit in and then make sure we are on cue and don't fluff our lines! It's all about *relationship*, man and God, God and Man, man and man. It's as simple as that.

So, hopefully, we are more or less on the same page here in our understanding of the difference between the original Biblical, Hebraic mindset and the worldly Greek mindset that currently defines not just our society, but also, in many ways, the Church itself.

To truly understand the ways of God we need to think Hebraically. At the heart of this is to always put God, not man, at the centre of everything.

But seek first his kingdom and his righteousness, and all these things will be given to you as well. (Matthew 6:33)

To do this we apply three rules, simple rules, but at the very heart of Hebraic thinking. They are the following:

1. *Does God get the Glory?* We can only answer this if we have a true understanding of God's character and desires. We have to make sure we have a true image of God and not one influenced by the devil's deception, or coloured by our feelings or influenced by the paganism of platonic thinking (from the dualistic teachings of Plato, where the spiritual and the physical are separated).

Are you honouring God?

2. *Are you a good witness to the world?* We can only answer this if we have a clear grip on what influences us. Is Jesus at the centre of our life, rather than personal ambition or agenda? Are we truly Hebraic in our lifestyle? Are we people of action or people of words?

Are you reflecting Jesus?

3. *Are you acting in accordance with Holy Scripture, correctly interpreted?* We can only answer this if we read God's Word without personal agenda and with proper tools, rather than the 'spiritualising' of the text or the 'rationalising' of Holy Scripture.

Are you engaging with the Holy Spirit?

These are good tools, easy to remember – as they are just the Trinity in action – and quite logical in their application.

It is now time to get a bit personal …

Shalom and Ra   6

In that twilight world between sleep and awakening, when the last wisps of dreamland fade, something within me often stalls, before my engines rev up. It can be a sense of well-being, or it can be a sense of dread. It's only a transient feeling, but it can add flavour to the rest of the day, so it is significant enough to think about.

And here's what I'm thinking. When everything in your world just clicks and seems to be in harmony, then you have reached a form of *shalom* in your life and, in my case, it's reflected as my sense of well-being when I wake up and prepare for the day ahead. Yet, in order to wake up with a sense of dread, I only need one or two things to be misfiring. Achieving *ra* (chaos, unease and disruption) is a lot easier than achieving *shalom*, I have found. Just one or two aspects of my life that are less than perfect is all that is needed for ra to reign. How on earth do pastors manage to sleep at all? It's the same for me when I'm writing books. Instinctively I know that the book is finished when, in terms of the content, there is complete *shalom* in my spirit and all vestiges of *ra* have dissipated.

So *ra* is a more natural state for us human beings, burdened as we are by our fallen natures and the fallen natures of those around us.

For the creation was subjected to frustration, not by its own choice, but by the will of the one who subjected it, in hope that the creation itself will be liberated from its bondage to decay and brought into the freedom and glory of the children of God. (Romans 8:20-21)

To achieve shalom in our lives, even in those of us who are already redeemed, there has to be a desire. For the redeemed, of course, it is not as central to our purpose as reaching others with the Gospel, however the Lord has led us in this task. Living in shalom should not be the main priority, but a wonderfully welcome result of the Christian life. If we are honestly fulfilling God's purpose in our life, then, as we shall see, we will have shalom and, indeed, this peacefulness and contentment should be a reflection to the outside world of Jesus living within us and, therefore, a great witness to unbelievers.

There are some Christians I know that just radiate *shalom*. They project such peacefulness even when you know that their lives are not that easy. These are people who have found *shalom* among the storms in their lives, who have entered into such a partnership with Jesus, that they have allowed him to calm these storms. This, after all, is one of the offers he makes for us:

"Come to me, all you who are weary and burdened, and I will give you rest. Take my yoke upon you and learn from me, for I am gentle and humble in heart, and you will find rest for your souls. For my yoke is easy and my burden is light." (Matthew 11:28-30)

But – oh dear – there are others who radiate *ra*, who bring chaos, misunderstandings, division wherever they go. Unfortunately and sadly, there are some Christians who fit this description. Brutal words may be needed for this latter case, as my advice would be to avoid them like the plague, otherwise they can drag you down and squeeze any shalom you may already have out of you. *How unchristian*, you may say, but I'm thinking of the Kingdom here, not our individual well-being, as these people, however they have got to where they are, could well be unwitting agents of Satan, sent to disrupt ministries. Of course, on the other hand, these people do need help and you will find that they attract sincere Christians who try to help them, out of the very best intentions. Unless you have direct leading and a calling to counsel these people, I would advise you to stay away, especially if God is doing great things in your life at the moment.

I urge you, brothers and sisters, to watch out for those who cause divisions and put obstacles in your way that are contrary to the teaching you have learned. Keep away from them. (Romans 16:17)

Then, of course, there are those who bring ra on purpose and knowingly. There are many warnings against such people:

For false messiahs and false prophets will appear and perform great signs and wonders to deceive, if possible, even the elect. (Matthew 24:24)

For the time will come when people will not put up with sound doctrine. Instead, to suit their own desires, they will gather around them a great number of teachers to say what their itching ears want to hear. They will turn their ears away from the truth and turn aside to myths. (2 Timothy 4:3-4)

Watch out for false prophets. They come to you in sheep's clothing, but inwardly they are ferocious wolves. By their fruit you will recognize them. Do people pick grapes from thorn bushes, or figs from thistles? (Matthew 7:15-16)

But there were also false prophets among the people, just as there will be false teachers among you. They will secretly introduce destructive heresies, even denying the sovereign Lord who bought them—bringing swift destruction on themselves. Many will follow their depraved conduct and will bring the way of truth into disrepute. In their greed these teachers will exploit you with fabricated stories. Their condemnation has long been hanging over them, and their destruction has not been sleeping. (2 Peter 2:1-3)

So, be vigilant, be alert. We need *shalom* in our lives.

The starting point, of course, is when Jesus enters our life. We will now explore a few aspects of this in our next section.

PART TWO
The Shalom of Salvation

Deplorables? 7

Think of the person you'd least like to reach with the Gospel (be honest now, we all have a nemesis out there, however we may deny it). I have someone in mind and it deeply shames me even to entertain such an unhelpful and self-condemning notion. But honesty has its downside, so I am giving us all a chance to redeem ourselves here.

Take that person and (in your mind's eye) sit them on a chair facing you. Now comes the interesting bit. We are going to strip them down (tastefully) to the basics. First, physicalities. Remove their gender (especially if they have adopted one of the more exotic varieties), their age, their appearance, even the aspects of their personality that you may find annoying. Next jettison any emotional response they stir up in you. Next come spiritual attachments, known and unknown, acknowledged and denied. These can be religious allegiances, but they can also be spiritual blockages, even unsavoury attachments, such as those connected to freemasonry, witchcraft, compulsive behaviour, or addictions.

What do we have left? The *person*, unplugged, just a lost soul quivering under the spotlight, the core of their very being, all other layers stripped away. And what does that soul need more than anything else? *Jesus, pure and simple.* And there's where your evangelism comes in because if we can view our worst enemy in this way, then everyone else in the world will just slip into place.

Why was this exercise necessary? Think of Jeremy

Corbyn (or anyone else of similar profile). Strip away the wizened old 'social justice warrior' persona and ignore any emotions he may provoke regarding his negativity towards Israel and look beyond the clutch that Marxism has on him, strengthened over years of devotion to this flawed ideal. Now look at him, a lost soul in an old man's body, someone who has followed a defective path and is seemingly a million miles away from where God would want him to be. Now think about loving him into the Kingdom.

By extension, think of the millions of aborted babies, killed through their inconvenience to others, or the foot soldiers (cannon fodder) of countless wars, slaughtered unthinkingly at the whim of the strategy of others, or those born with physical or mental deficiencies, considered 'less than human', or the inconveniently old, betrayed by the entropy of time, or the millions who are trapped into following a religion that would doom them to destruction, or those sexually confused on a 'pride' march, taught by others to celebrate their differences and to define themselves by their gender identity. All souls as worthy of God's Kingdom as anyone else, but overlooked because of physical, emotional or spiritual factors, because they are *not like us* and therefore a problem for others to deal with. God's Kingdom is not an old boys' club, or a 'members only' exclusive society, or any other reflection of the world's Kingdom. It's a place of true diversity, inhabited by the choice of God, not man, however that pans out theologically.

Jesus could have ignored the lepers, prostitutes, tax collectors and other social pariahs and *stuck to his own*, nice provincial Jewish boys who would look like him and share a common background. But he didn't.

But the Pharisees and the teachers of the law who belonged to their sect complained to his disciples, "Why do you eat and drink with tax collectors and sinners?" Jesus answered them, "It is not the healthy who need a doctor, but the sick. I have not come to call the righteous, but sinners to repentance." (Luke 5:30-32)

He was in the business of 'saving souls' and so should we be. We are not expected to judge others, to focus on 'the sin', but rather we must embrace the mindset that all are sinners and all have fallen short and, although we may perceive some sins to be worse than others, we must refrain from adding our prejudices and 'righteous anger' and just consider that naked soul sitting, quivering, on that chair. God will judge, not us:

There is only one Lawgiver and Judge, the one who is able to save and destroy. But you—who are you to judge your neighbour? (James 4:12)

This is a tricky one, especially when confronted with extremes of gender identity and everything within us winces with indignation. And it shows. They know it and will do all that they can to provoke you into a reaction, even if you are just showing it in your eyes. Great self-control is needed here and perhaps we should remind ourselves of the model we should aspire to:

But the fruit of the Spirit is love, joy, peace, forbearance, kindness, goodness, faithfulness, gentleness and self-control. Against such things there is no law. (Galatians 5:22-23)

Well that's easy for Paul to say, we may think. *He was never confronted by a bricklayer with stubble dressed in a miniskirt and stockings!* But, then again, he surely saw sights far worse, in the corrupt and licentious Roman culture in which he lived and preached. So we evangelise without prejudice, confident that God will put the people in our paths that He can trust us with and that He will give us all that we need to get the job done. All we need to do is rely on Him and not any judgement that comes from the flesh. It's all about practice, really, so now may be a good time to prepare yourself for the next person God will bring before you ... perhaps sooner than you think!

On a recent trip to Jerusalem (more of that later) I was confronted by a surprising sight. A group of Muslims in religious garb had congregated on the upper steps leading down to the Western Wall. It was a Shabbat, the holiest time of the week. After a short talk the group proceeded down the steps, the ladies to the Wall and the men to the underground tunnels to the left of the Wall. I followed the men into the tunnels, where their group squeezed single-file past the collection of religious Jews, congregated around small platforms, reading from Torah scrolls, or swaying backwards and forwards in prayer on rickety chairs. The Muslims silently and without fuss did a circuit of the first long chamber, then left the tunnel area. Again I followed them as they started to leave the Western Wall plaza and heard them speak among themselves. They were English, there were recognisable accents, from Manchester to London. I was intrigued and spoke to them.

Here's an observation. There was no appreciable interaction between the Muslims and any Jewish observers, despite any perceived feelings of 'enemy infiltration'. There were just a few curious glances in their direction as they moved through the crowd, yet no hostility, from either direction. I had a great conversation with them, they were just ordinary folk who just happened to be religious Muslims. They were acting just like any other tourist, curious to see how others live and worship and nothing more. Yet, in accordance to media stereotypes, they were the 'alien invader', a natural enemy to the Jewish people. Of course, a short conversation is never going to achieve full mutual understanding, but sometimes we must look beyond the *form* (the 'battle dress') and even the perceived *function* (their interpretation of Islamic theology) and ... at the person beneath the hijab (women) and thaub (men), at the soul given life by the beating heart beneath the robe.

And there it is. Most of us would probably be happiest if God only sent nice people across our path, people we feel most connected to, people we may feel best equipped to evangelise. Our God ain't that predictable, He isn't that polite English gentle-god exuding fairness and bonhomie, bowling safe balls to ensure a fair game and a pleasant conclusion. No, like any loving Father, He stretches us, pushes us, takes us to our limit and thus equips us to run the human race, with all the obstacles and setbacks that come with the territory. All we have to be is willing to trust Him.

So the next time you open your front door to a dishevelled and slightly whiffy 'street person', perhaps it's not just to help them out with a few coppers from your loose change?

The Shalom of Salvation   8

Surely the greatest shalom of all, the completeness of being reconciled to our Maker.

"See, I will create new heavens and a new earth. The former things will not be remembered, nor will they come to mind." (Isaiah 65:17)

A new start. That's what we desire, a return to that true shalom in that Garden of Delights (Eden), representing a full renewal of heaven and earth. In the meantime, there's work to do. We are all called to this work, as the Great Commission (Matthew 28) tells us, even if we may not be the front-line warriors. We must never forget the incredible act of grace that has allowed you and me, undeserving souls, into the Kingdom, with the promise of a life with meaning and an after-life of complete joy. With that realisation comes the awesome responsibility that *it's not just about us,* there's a whole world of other undeserving people out there who need saving too.

And some of them, in our eyes, may be extremely undeserving, as we explored in the previous chapter. We looked beyond the form, we even looked beyond the function, we drilled down to the very essence of that person before us, *their very soul.*

Finally, one thing that often bothers me is the occasional attitude from some Christians. Call me 'over-sensitive' but when I hear a Christian exclaim, after hearing about another atrocity or perversion in our society, *Come Lord Jesus, Come Now*, what they can be really saying is; *take me home, I've had enough, the rest of them can go to Hell!*

Seems a bit harsh and I'm sure they don't really mean this but the reality is that a Christian is assured of a glorious future, but all those 'Left behind' can have little confidence about their future! Shouldn't we have the attitude of wanting to save souls until our dying breath, or is this just for those we consider as the professional 'evangelists' among us? The focus turns to us and how much we sometimes obsess on our own salvation and reward, at the expense of others. It is time to get serious.

OK, so we're saved, we are redeemed, we have the shalom of salvation. So far so good, as I fully expect my readership to fall within the realm of the Kingdom of God, where *salvation* is a given, not an issue. There is, of course, a lot more that can be said on this topic, but that is for other books. For us, this is just the beginning of our story into the Shalom of God. So ... what next?

PART THREE
The Shalom of Unity

Finding ourselves   9

Here's the ideal, as set down in Scripture:

Just as a body, though one, has many parts, but all its many parts form one body, so it is with Christ. For we were all baptized by one Spirit so as to form one body–whether Jews or Gentiles, slave or free–and we were all given the one Spirit to drink. Even so the body is not made up of one part but of many.

Now if the foot should say, "Because I am not a hand, I do not belong to the body," it would not for that reason stop being part of the body. And if the ear should say, "Because I am not an eye, I do not belong to the body," it would not for that reason stop being part of the body. If the whole body were an eye, where would the sense of hearing be? If the whole body were an ear, where would the sense of smell be? But in fact God has placed the parts in the body, every one of them, just as he wanted them to be. If they were all one part, where would the body be? As it is, there are many parts, but one body.

The eye cannot say to the hand, "I don't need you!" And the head cannot say to the feet, "I don't need you!" On the contrary, those parts of the body that seem to be weaker are indispensable, and the parts that we think are less honourable we treat with special honour. And the parts that are unpresentable are treated with special modesty, while our presentable parts need no special treatment. But God has put the body together, giving greater honour to the parts that lacked it, so that there should be no division in the body, but that its parts should have equal concern for each other. If one part suffers, every part suffers with it; if one part is honoured, every part rejoices with it.

Now you are the body of Christ, and each one of you is a part of it. And God has placed in the church first of all apostles, second prophets, third teachers, then miracles, then gifts of healing, of helping, of guidance, and of different kinds of tongues. Are all apostles? Are all prophets? Are all teachers? Do all work miracles? Do all have gifts of healing? Do all speak in tongues? Do all interpret? Now eagerly desire the greater gifts. (1 Corinthians 12:12-31)

Now let's speak frankly. If our human bodies operated in the same way as our current implementation of the Body of Christ, we would basically be big fleshy heads scampering around aimlessly on a myriad of tiny fingers. Unbalanced, ineffective, top-heavy, with most of the body relegated to the most menial of tasks, irrespective of their God-given abilities and the head huffing and puffing away and getting nowhere fast. This is what happens when we human beings are put in charge! The plan was a good one, but the implementation is often quite lacking.

As the passage tells us, God has constructed the human body with great care and intelligence, with eyes, ears, hands and feet in the correct places according to their function, many parts all working together. No part is to be deemed more important than any other, with each part respecting and honouring all others. Then the focus turns to us, *the Body of Christ*. The first observation is that all of us Christians belong to this "Body", which means that we *all* have a purpose. There seems to be a hierarchy of functions and we should set our sights on the greater gifts, but – and this is important – *the choice is not ours, it is God's.*

We have different gifts, according to the grace given to each of us. If your gift is prophesying, then prophesy in accordance with your faith; if it is serving, then serve; if it is teaching, then teach; if it is to encourage, then give encouragement; if it is giving, then give generously; if it is to lead, do it diligently; if it is to show mercy, do it cheerfully. (Romans 12:6-8)

Our gifts are in accordance to God's grace. We can *desire* the greater gifts for ourselves or others in our congregations, but the decision is not ours. We are equipped in accordance to the function that God has planned for us.

So does it follow that we all operate in the gifts that God has allocated to us? I would suggest that this doesn't always happen, or that it happens but not in a timely manner. I was recently teaching a small Bible class on these matters and one gentleman introduced himself, a man who, when he was living in Zimbabwe was a pastor and a planter of many churches. Now he lives a humble life in Belfast and dutifully occupies the pews of his local church, who have no idea of the giftings they have failed to acknowledge. How many other hidden jewels are lost in the pews because churches don't have the system or the will to unearth them?

This is a good point to consider something intrinsic to Hebraic thinking, in that it concentrates on what we have been put on this earth for, rather than navel-gazing and inward thinking. It is something that turns Greek thinking right on its head. It is the concept of *form* and *function*. It arises from a view of things from the perspective of God, rather than the Greek concept of man being at the centre of everything. For God everything in Creation has a purpose.

The LORD works out everything to its proper end – even the wicked for a day of disaster. (Proverbs 16:4)

For in him all things were created: things in heaven and on earth, visible and invisible, whether thrones or powers or rulers or authorities; all things have been created through him and for him. (Colossians 1:16)

For we are God's handiwork, created in Christ Jesus to do good works, which God prepared in advance for us to do. (Ephesians 2:10)

Those first believers were characterised by the role they had to play, their purposes in the great scheme of things. They all had gifts, in accordance with God's plan for each individual life.

We have different gifts, according to the grace given to each of us. If your gift is prophesying, then prophesy in accordance with your faith; if it is serving, then serve; if it is teaching, then teach; if it is to encourage, then give encouragement; if it is giving, then give generously; if it is to lead, do it diligently; if it is to show mercy, do it cheerfully. (Romans 12:6-8)

Of course, this Scripture was directed at them, but it also applies to us now. But do we really take it on board?

Everything in Creation (including you and me) should be identified by its purpose, or *function*, as well as its physical appearance, its *form*. In our culture, it is *form* that rules, we observe objects, we use them, we collect them, we are them. We're comfortable with nouns. In God's Kingdom, verbs are more important. Even the Hebrew language, the language of most of the Bible, is a *verb-orientated language*, a language of action, of doing things.

This really is *thinking differently*. When we meet a Christian friend we should be wondering what good works God has prepared in advance for them to do. What are their gifts *according to the grace given to them?* What is their function in God's Kingdom? When we meet an unbeliever, we should wonder what role God may have for us to introduce them into God's kingdom. It's not so much *who we are*, but rather *what we do*, that is important to God.

For I desire mercy, not sacrifice, and acknowledgment of God rather than burnt offerings. (Hosea 6:6)

God is not keen on our dry rituals or disengaged

worship, but would rather see our faith in action. Here's another expression of that idea:

If anyone has material possessions and sees a brother or sister in need but has no pity on them, how can the love of God be in that person? Dear children, let us not love with words or speech but with actions and in truth. (1 John 3:17-18)

God is not interested so much in our knowledge of Scripture as our openness to Scripture changing our lives. He prefers our engagement with Him over our knowledge of Him. He may laugh (I think) at some of us who proudly claim the *office* of pastor, prophet, apostle etc. but don't *function* in those gifts. He may laugh even more (and cry) at our attempts at creating strategies for fundraising that have been borrowed from the world, when all we have to do is pray for these funds. Perhaps He cries at the mechanistic or even ritualistic way we may do our evangelism, with the accent on reciting creeds, set prayers and spiritual laws, rather than a sincere desire for a relationship with Jesus. Similarly with the use of rosaries, relics, amulets, icons and crosses, when all He desires is a simple direct faith in Him. Sermons, scriptural songs or even books are ineffectual unless we can discern God speaking to us through these activities.

We put the accent on healing services, evangelistic rallies, worship concerts and huge prayer vigils, while all God wants to do is meet us individually and for us to experience Him. Of course He will meet us at these places, even where manipulation and emotionalism are employed, because He will honour our search. But we can save a lot of time and money by just finding a quiet (or even noisy) place simply to meet with Him.

It is form and function. *You yourself* are the form, but *you in relationship with God* is your function, which is to be greatly preferred. You may be Fred Smith, but God is more interested in *Fred-the-encourager-of-those-who-are-struggling*. We all need to find out what that function is and we will now go deeper ...

Finding our function   10

Here's something that I believe is so important, yet I've never seen it discussed outside architecture studios. We just had a taster of it in the previous chapter, but its reach goes far beyond, finding expressions within life's rich tapestry.

Plato made much of his theory of "Forms", which he saw as ideal representations of everything we can see, touch and even think about in our physical world, from chairs and diamonds to geometric shapes or even concepts such as goodness. Inasmuch as he was a pagan philosopher, writing from a Greek mindset and detached from an understanding of his Creator, his theory couldn't have been more wrong, particularly as it gave rise to the dualism that has been a scourge of humanity ever since. Rather than existing as ephemeral objects floating about in the ether, *forms* are very much a part of the real, physical world. Here is the only definition I can find of them, in relation to *function*, quoted by designer of designers, Louis Henry Sullivan, the father of the skyscraper:

"Whether it be the sweeping eagle in his flight, or the open apple-blossom, the toiling work-horse, the blithe swan, the branching oak, the winding stream at its base, the drifting clouds, over all the coursing sun, **form ever follows function**, *and this is the law. Where function does not change, form does not change. The granite rocks, the ever-brooding hills, remain for ages; the lightning lives, comes into shape, and dies, in a twinkling. It is the pervading law of all things organic and inorganic, of all things*

*physical and metaphysical, of all things human and all things superhuman, of all true manifestations of the head, of the heart, of the soul, that the life is recognizable in its expression, that **form ever follows function**. This is the law."*

This is function in terms of *design*, rather than purpose, so perhaps we have to discard this scenario and redefine what 'form and function' are in God's eyes? Now it is time for honesty. When I first started writing about form and function, introduced three years ago in *Hebraic Church*, all I remember is waking up at 2am in a bed in Exmouth with "form and function" in my mind. It appears that it must have been a revelation, as I can find no source anywhere for the ideas explained in that book, some of which you've already read at the end of the previous chapter. That may seem like a touch of arrogance, but it's me trying to be modestly honest. I challenge you to find any other writer touching on this subject. It would be wonderful to see some reinforcement on these matters. But God continues to exercise me on this and a whole new world of possibilities has suddenly opened up. Let me explain ...

As well as being our guide for reconciliation with God, *the Bible*, God's instruction manual for mankind, speaks to me as a book of tasks, designed to teach us in the way we should live and act. Doctrine is good for the mind, the poetry is good for the spirit, but, unless this book can inspire us to be God's witness in a godless world, then we're missing something, we're not complete, we're *not living in shalom*.

Here are just a few of the lessons we learn from the actions and thoughts of others:

"Abraham believed God, and it was credited to him as righteousness." (Romans 4:3)

Abraham's belief resulted in actions. He didn't just

debate with God about the possibility of allowing his son to be sacrificed, he schlepped him up the mountain to carry out the deed. This should inspire us to act on any instructions from God, even when they claw at our spirits.

Be strong and very courageous. Be careful to obey all the law my servant Moses gave you; do not turn from it to the right or to the left, that you may be successful wherever you go. (Joshua 1:7)

Joshua was given instructions directly from God, concerning what he had to do for him and his people to prosper, in the land they had inherited. Everything was going to hang on Joshua's response to these instructions, it was all about practice not theory. We, of course, must take note of this and also live our lives according to God's Word.

In his distress he sought the favour of the LORD his God and humbled himself greatly before the God of his ancestors. And when he prayed to him, the LORD was moved by his entreaty and listened to his plea; so he brought him back to Jerusalem and to his kingdom. Then Manasseh knew that the LORD is God. (2 Chronicles 33:12-13)

The most evil king of Judah had turned to the Lord and mended his ways, even throwing out all of the pagan altars. His repentance was genuine and God forgave him. He was saved by his actions, just as his previous actions had condemned him. This gives us an amazing picture of the God of grace and should encourage us to realise that, if the most evil king of Judah can be forgiven then so can we, as long as our repentance is genuine and accompanied by actions.

Abraham was a clan leader, Joshua a military commander and Manasseh was a king. These are their forms, their identity, but their forms did not define them. It was their individual functions, their deeds and actions that grafted them into the pages of the Bible.

Abraham was no ordinary clan leader, he was the one who left the safety of his home town and travelled to a strange land, answering the call of a God who had much for him to do. His function was defined by his name, Abraham, *Avraham*, "Father of many nations". He was to be the great example of a faith-filled man, one who received a legacy, implied by his name, that would reverberate through history.

Joshua wasn't your average military commander. He was to oversee the conquering of the Land of Canaan and was under no illusion that this was only going to be achieved if he and his army were to comply with God's plan. Again this is implied by his name, Joshua, *Jehoshua*, "God is Salvation". God will save His people, physically, through conquest, at the hand of His servant Joshua.

Manasseh wasn't a typical king of Judah, he was by far the worst. His name means "to forget", which is a curious but fitting legacy for a man who, although he repented at the very end, created much havoc in the fifty odd preceding years! Best forgotten, really.

These three examples, out of the hundreds that we could have investigated, show a group of individuals who played their part in the great drama of the Bible. They each had a unique function and it was interesting how their names reflected an aspect of their function. That's how the Bible does it, the best example being Jesus himself, his Hebrew name, *Yeshua*, meaning "salvation". His chief function in his life (and death) was to save his people, something stated quite clearly (but lost in most English translations) in Matthew 1:21:

She will give birth to a son, and you are to give him the name Jesus (Yeshua, Salvation), because he will save his people from their sins.

The Bible features a string of *functioning* men and women, be they prophets, priests, kings, poets, military leaders, farmers, slaves and so on. If a new Bible were to be written featuring the exploits of Christians living in the UK in the 21st Century, what a different book that could be! It would be a book of exciting conferences, great music-soaked celebrations, dramas in village squares and the odd vicar caught with his pants down. To be honest, in comparison with the heady days of the ancient Jews, we don't get up to much really. Of course this is not a fair comparison, as the Bible is not being re-written, the first is perfectly adequate for all of our needs and, if God had a purpose for our current generation, other than the treading-water that we seem to be doing, then He would empower us to be men and women of great function and purpose. This doesn't mean that we shouldn't have aspirations, though, because we don't know what lies ahead of us, in a world becoming increasingly madder.

We feel safe in our Christian "forms", as redeemed Children of God, and many of us would prefer basking in our grace-fuelled blessed state, as we wait for heaven to beckon. This is a wrong attitude and, I'm afraid, our forefathers in the faith are much to blame. In particular, one of the most influential Church Fathers, Augustine. He was extremely influenced by Plato, with the idea that the *physical*, material world is bad (or evil) and that the *spiritual*, heavenly world is good and to be eagerly sought. To be blunt, it's a death cult masquerading as a philosophy of life and these early Christian thinkers had a theology thoroughly infiltrated by it. In his book, the *City of God*, Augustine consoled his readers that one should not concern oneself with such worldly matters as the destruction of Rome, the *City of Man*, but should rather look heavenwards at the "city yet to come", the *City of God*, the New Jerusalem of the Book of Revelation. On the face of it this is a noble mission, a thoroughly Christian pursuit, but to measure the true worth of a book is to examine its legacy. What sort of influence did the *City of God* have on those who read it, on those who converted its words into action?

It was a very large book, full of challenging ideas and it was to be read in many different ways, by different people. Some saw the book as a handbook for a *theocratic* society, governed by the Church, or those appointed by it, whether king or pope, as the best way forward. Others took a different view. By holding out hope for the Christian, by saying in effect, *don't worry about the mess in this world you have to live in, there's a better world to come*, many saw, in these words, justification for the acceptance of a life of disappointment, deprivation and disaster as *there's better to come in the next life!* As the publication of this book was swiftly followed by the *Dark Ages*, there's a strong possibility that this seminal book from the most influential Christian thinker in a society that considered itself a Christian one, had something to do with it!

The new kind of Christians, after the fall (of Rome), had little interest in their bodies as such. They cared about the health of their souls. They had no interest in consumption. They could lose their reputation rather than gain it for possessing wealth in a society where poverty was next to godliness. Roman wealth was replaced by Christian poverty. (A History of Knowledge, Charles Van Doren p.96, Ballantine Books 1992).

Just as we, living in the affluent West in the 21st Century, believe that progress is determined by the number of cars in the garage, the size of our plasma screens or the availability of exotic foreign spices in our supermarkets, our 10th Century friends would have considered themselves living in enlightenment, devoting their lives to the well-being of their souls, that precious commodity, their ticket to a good afterlife. In a way, perhaps they got it right! The trouble is that their objective may have been a good one, but the way of getting there was eminently flawed.

Sacraments were the way into Heaven at that time. Ordinary folk couldn't understand a word of the liturgies in their local church, as it was all in Latin. Neither did they have a correct balanced understanding of Jesus, as Bibles were just not available for the common man and, if they had been, no-one would have been able to read them. Yet they were told that if they followed the actions dictated by the sacraments they would be alright. Sacraments controlled their daily lives. Baptism at the start of life was absolutely necessary, as was regular penance – confessing your sins (with payment to the church) and regular Holy Communion. Real, considered, saving faith didn't come into it. You were "saved" through your actions, as if the act itself was sufficient. It is a sad and sobering thought to consider how many from those times had a nasty shock in the next world. You must also wonder whether someone with an incomplete, even false, understanding of the historical Jesus and the purpose of his death is any better off than an ignorant native in the heart of the Amazon jungle. Only the Lord has the answer to that one.

It was "salvation by forms", or just a *form* of salvation, not a real one. It was expecting God to be satisfied by just lip-service to the sacraments, a series of rituals, external observances, that may have been underpinned by functional truth, but which had become forms. For instance, Holy Communion as a Biblical act of remembrance of what Jesus achieved for us is a sacred and meaningful act, but not so much when it has become a meaningless duty just for appearance's sake, or as a passport to eternal life.

Sacraments are still alive and well in our modern Church and one's use of them needs to be dictated by individual consciences, rather than edicts from church hierarchies. If they are a reflection of one's relationship with Jesus then that's good, but if they are a reflection of one's relationship with the Church, then that could be a very different matter.

Finding the Church   11

We live in a world of forms, objects, nouns and things and every one of them belongs to God.

The LORD has made all for Himself, Yes, even the wicked for the day of doom. (Proverbs 16:4 NKJV)

Every form has been made for a purpose or function, God's purpose. Even the wicked have a self-created purpose, tied up in a future described as a *day of doom*.

We see a world of forms, God sees a world of possibilities. Every form has a function, or intended function, but sometimes we fail to notice this. Here are a couple of examples, just to whet your appetite and get you *thinking differently*.

Consider *old people*, deemed useless to society at an arbitrary age, depending on some fiscal algorithm, currently 66 years and 2 months for me, according to the official government website. *Go off and tend your garden, you are no use for us any more,* is one attitude. Tell that to Moses, Noah, Samuel and other Biblical giants, reaching their peak of usefulness to God at an age when our current society retires them off and consigns them to 'heaven's waiting room'. Tell that to some of our greatest preachers and teachers, who functioned right up to their dying breath.

Is not wisdom found among the aged? Does not long life bring understanding? Job 12:12

What the world sees is a deteriorating body, the slowing of limbs, the failing of sight and hearing. But it doesn't look where it often really counts, with the lifetime of accumulated wisdom that can still be shared, the *true function*. It is well for us to remember the folly of Rehoboam:

But Rehoboam rejected the advice the elders gave him and consulted the young men who had grown up with him and were serving him. He asked them, "What is your advice? (1 Kings 12:8-9)

He chose testosterone over the 'test of time' and, as a result, doomed himself and his kingdom. Of course, one should not create doctrine out of a single example, but it's a tale worth telling about where we should turn to for wisdom.

Perhaps those youthful advisors are the equivalent of those who currently clog up the digital ether with 'twitter wisdom', where the simple formula seems to be that the more 'followers' accrued, the more vacuous or insignificant or harmful is the 'wisdom'. The top two twitter accounts in terms of followers are Katy Perry and Justin Bieber, each with over 100 million followers. One hundred million people are feeding from the 'wisdom' of a couple of millionaire singers, both benefiting from a pleasing *form*, in terms of physical attractiveness and singing ability, but with less wisdom, I suspect, than a hamster on a treadmill (though both, interestingly, have tenuous Christian connections). Do you really need Justin and Katy to tell you how to vote, what to think about the climate, immigration, or other issues? Yet many of our youngsters do, as if a pretty face implies an insightful mind, to say nothing of matters of ethics and morality.

A politician will pat the head of a baby (as long as a camera is nearby) to look good in the tabloids and to improve his approval rating. He will also be seen to be in favour of popularist issues and in opposition to those deemed unsavoury. And it's a point of principal to support issues promoted by their own political party and oppose those promoted by the opposition, whatever their conscience may be telling him. This is all *form* and image and this, incredibly, is the driving force of our democracy, the trust we put in these people. Yet the *function* can tell a very different story. One web definition of a politician had them as *a person who acts in a manipulative and devious way, typically to gain advancement within an organization.* Comedian Rodney Dangerfield once said, *"the way my luck is running, if I was a politician I would be honest".* The function of a politician is to be seen to be putting things right, even if nothing really changes, or it is just a short-term fix to achieve an instant burst of approval.

Of course we all have a propensity to behave in this way, this is why the system is allowed to continue. In our western society, our interactions with others often don't reflect our inner motivations. A politician or celebrity makes an unwise statement and is forced to make a public apology. This is just a form, a gesture, it doesn't necessarily equate with contriteness. A celebrity may declare they are a Christian by wearing a cross, attending the odd trendy worship service or uttering a vaguely Christian sound-byte, but they still usually function very differently in terms of lifestyle. Form and function are often worlds apart.

They claim to know God, but by their actions they deny him. They are detestable, disobedient and unfit for doing anything good. (Titus 1:16)

We live in a world of forms, of appearances, of gestures, of image, of identity. It manifests itself as fashion, public relations, pageantry, worthiness, 'virtue signalling' and so on. This is the 'kingdom of the world' and we are not called to judge it, but rather help lost souls to escape from it into the Kingdom of God. The big issue is when both

Kingdoms intersect and the Church is pulled into the mindset of the world. It is happening and increasingly so. We have read the following Scripture enough times:

But mark this: There will be terrible times in the last days. People will be lovers of themselves, lovers of money, boastful, proud, abusive, disobedient to their parents, ungrateful, unholy, without love, unforgiving, slanderous, without self-control, brutal, not lovers of the good, treacherous, rash, conceited, lovers of pleasure rather than lovers of God– having a form of godliness but denying its power. Have nothing to do with such people. (2 Timothy 3:1-5)

It's the *form of godliness* we need to beware of, form without function. It is saying to the world, *look at me, I'm a child of the King of Heaven*, but doing nothing to demonstrate it ...

<Controversial statement alert!>

This may be where much of the Western Church is right now.

I am not saying this lightly, for a convenient sound-byte. Sadly the evidence is increasingly pointing to a Church that has veered completely away from *the Maker's original instructions*. Let me explain ...

The Church began with that small group of Jews in the Jerusalem Temple receiving a huge outpouring of Holy Spirit, birthing a new movement that would spread the Gospel message of Jesus Christ and help save as much of the world as they were capable of reaching. The Church was, and still is, the empowered people of God i.e. you and me. The Greek word in question is *ekklesia*, interestingly a feminine noun, fitting for a people described elsewhere as 'the bride of Christ'. Its literal translation is "called out ones", an apt description of what a Christian was meant to be.

In one of the very first English translations, that by

William Tyndale in 1525, the word was translated reasonably accurately and succinctly as "congregation", as in "a group of people". In 1611, the King James Version (KJV), the first mass produced English translation, instead chose to translate *ekklesia* as "Church". This word came from the Old English *cirice*, which took the meaning of 'a religious building'. So why is *ekklesia*, in 115 out of 118 instances in the New Testament, referring to a building, or an ecclesiastical institution represented by the building? *Politics, my dear Watson, politics!*

Ever since the Emperor Constantine had initiated a church-building programme in 325 AD, ornate constructions, each outdoing the one before, began to spring up throughout the Empire, one of the first being St Peter's basilica in Rome. He also sent his mother, Helena, to the Middle East to "identify" the holy sites in Jerusalem and other places, so that more impressive church buildings could be built.

These churches and cathedrals became part of the phenomenon known as *Christendom*, a visible attempt to build Christ's kingdom on earth. It became a multinational organisation, with vast hierarchies, governed by the Pope and with access to unlimited riches and lands, as befitting a "kingdom". This was the visible "Church" in those days, a million miles away from God's intention:

Jesus said, *"My kingdom is not of this world. If it were, my servants would fight to prevent my arrest by the Jewish leaders. But now my kingdom is from another place."* (John 18:36)

King James I was a part of the system, protected by the doctrine of the "divine right of Kings" and, as such, took on the responsibility of ensuring that any other view of what the Church is meant to be will be unforthcoming, even if it were true. So *ekklesia* was translated in such a way as to re-inforce the status-quo and all was well in the Kingdom!

The truly sad thing is that subsequent Bible translations in more enlightened times have also chosen to 'toe the line.' Take 1 Corinthians 11:18, as an example:
For first of all, when ye come together in the church, I hear that there be divisions among you; and I partly believe it. (KJV)

Every other major English translation also translates *ekklesia* the King James way. I find that curious as surely accuracy of translation should trump political concerns in an era when the Church has lost most of its hold on secular society. Is it too revolutionary to translate the above as 'when ye come together as a congregation'?

So where has this got us in the light of my controversial statement, regarding the *form of godliness* of the Western Church today? Let us examine this in terms of form and function.

To the outside world, here is the *form* that the church currently takes: buildings (including non-traditional places such as sports halls etc), the organisations that run the buildings, denominations etc.

What about the perceived *functions* of the current Church? To keep the churches maintained, to pay church staff, to fulfil affairs of state, such as royal weddings, to look after an investment and property portfolio, to pay pensions for ex-employees, to take up seats in the House of Lords, to provide the odd sound-byte after a major disaster, or pressing issues. In short, the function of the mainstream Church in the UK can be described as *a national organisation with a remit to deal with religious matters.* Of course, the Church of England mostly springs to mind, but this is equally relevant to the Roman Catholics, Baptists, Methodists etc. and, to a lesser extent, even the independent groupings that sprung forth from the charismatic revival of the 1970s and 80s and have now become denominations in their own right.

Of course this function fits well with the "traditional" translation of *ekklesia*. It reinforces the image of a religious organisation rather than ... what it was created to be. Which brings us to the form of the original Church, of the Book of Acts.

= The *ekklesia*, the "called out ones". This is you and me, the Church.

And the *function?* To represent the Kingdom of God and promote the Gospel of Jesus Christ. That was the function at the birth of the "Church" and it's the function now. Nothing has changed, despite the efforts of Satan to thwart the work of God in the intervening centuries.

Now that we know what we are and what we are meant to do, it is time to explore our function and how we may achieve shalom, completeness, by doing so.

Finding Shalom   12

The Shalom of unity is what we should strive for as Christians. To do this, we need to be working together in unity:

How good and pleasant it is when God's people live together in unity! (Psalm 133:1)

It's not just good and pleasant, but entirely necessary:

I appeal to you, brothers and sisters, in the name of our Lord Jesus Christ, that all of you agree with one another in what you say and that there be no divisions among you, but that you be perfectly united in mind and thought. (1 Corinthians 1:10)

Let's be honest, we often could do better on this issue.

The first thing we should realise is that Paul is talking to the Church here. He is not talking to the "Church" as we currently define it. Can you imagine if he was? He would be asking the 40,000+ denominations to start working together and forget their differences! Just as well he's not talking to them then. He's talking to the Church, as originally defined, the *ekklesia*, you and me.

So we re-programme our minds and remove centuries of conditioning, telling us that the "Church" is basically a religious corporation, a vague controlling body on a higher plane, run by professionals and dog-collars! This is difficult, particularly for those who currently worship within the structures of a denomination, even if the local church expression gives the impression of independence.

Here is the problem and it's one that seems to be currently growing. Some Christians are beginning to feel uncomfortable within the current system. At Foundations we are used to mopping up Christians who have left (or have been asked to leave) their churches over "contentious" issues, usually over Israel. But this is different. The thinking tends to be on the lines of, *I don't feel on the same wavelength any more or I feel uncomfortable about some of the pronouncements made by my denomination or even I can't in all conscience stay in a church that compromises over ...*

There is no doubt that our society is changing, the cultural climate is becoming more restrictive and what we now say and do is under closer scrutiny than ever before. Now is the time for the Church to show unity, yet, here are some examples as representative of the problem at hand:

• The Church of England is torn over plans by The Episcopal Church (TEC) in the United States to remove the terms "husband" and "wife" from its marriage liturgy. The change is meant to make the church's marriage ceremonies more "gay-friendly." Gay and lesbian Episcopalians have complained that the language of the current liturgy is offensive and exclusionary. (Daily Telegraph 30/4/18)

• Transgender people are being encouraged to become Church of England vicars as bishops launch a diversity drive. Bishops in the diocese of Lichfield have issued new guidance to parishioners and clergy reminding them that LGBT people "can be called to roles of leadership and service in the local church". The guidance, titled "welcoming and honouring LGBT+ people", warns that the church's reputation as being unwelcoming towards gay and transgender people is stopping young people attending. (Daily Telegraph 26/5/18)

• The British Methodist Church, with the BDS movement, is distributing a questionnaire calling for a boycott of Israel. This is a significant step against Israel. It extends their 2010 partial boycott of "settlement" products. Now they are hitting all of Israel. (Jerusalem Post 16/10/13)

• There has been a deafening silence from all quarters of the established Church over the current rampant anti-Semitism in the actions of Jeremy Corbyn and the hard left in the Labour party. Yet clerics were all-a-tweetin' when Boris Johnson made a clumsy joke about burka wearers. Active tweeter, Justin Welby, has tweeted nothing on this issue during the height of the furore, which is disgraceful. (His excuse would be that the C of E wouldn't comment on 'political' matters, which is itself a 'political' statement). "Christian" anti-Semitism is, apparently live and kicking in the great halls of Ecclesiastica.

This is just for starters and just gives a taster of the wider problem. As the world sees these proclamations as the representatives of the *ekklesia*, is it no wonder that serious and worried Christians seek to distance themselves once and for all from those who will put the Biblical faith in Jesus Christ in disrepute?

As said earlier our *function* is to represent the Kingdom of God and promote the Gospel of Jesus Christ. If those who claim to speak up for us are not doing this faithfully, then it's time, perhaps, that we decided that they don't stick up for us anymore. This means that you will no longer have to be tarred with the same brush and have to explain to non-believers the latest proclamations from the established Church.

So, how will this work? Only God knows these things and His plans for us all may be very different. Here are some scenarios:

• You are happy and content in your local church.

It is a Bible based fellowship, linked to a local network and concentrates all of its efforts on the Gospel.

This has to be the ideal and the best working model in today's world. A group of like-minded Christians, hopefully united in mind and in thought.

- You are in a local expression of a major denomination. You are happy and content as the local leadership is strong and unafraid to contradict any nonsensical or unbiblical statements made by the denominational leaders.

As long as it remains this way, then you probably feel comfortable. But you must always be wary of a change in policy if the local leadership changes, or if it changes its mind.

- You are in a church grouping that has a voice in society ... and you are not sure you like what they are saying on your behalf.

This is where the rubber hits the road because you have a decision to make, along with hundreds of others too. *Do I stay or do I go?* Only one Person can help here because it is not 'do I want to leave the church', it is rather, *where does God want me to be?* It can be no other way.

Here is the reading at my baptism that has really defined my life, correcting me and blessing me:

Trust in the LORD with all your heart and lean not on your own understanding; in all your ways submit to him, and he will make your paths straight. (Proverbs 3:5-6)

It must ever be this way, otherwise you are just following your heart, your feelings, your instincts, all that veers towards the subjective. And we must never forget that leaving a fellowship will always involve other people, real flesh and blood people who can be hurt. And, after all, the *shalom of unity* is really about other people, as we shall now discuss.

It is back to form and function. Our form is *ekklesia*, the "called out ones", not the called out *one*, but a joint enterprise with others, some of whom will be very different to you in terms of background, experience, age, culture, race and so on. But we are all connected by this invisible thread, like a loosely-stitched garment, with a shared function to represent the Kingdom of God and promote the Gospel of Jesus Christ.

Now, before we move on, create a mental picture of the following, of how Paul describes us in Ephesians 2:20-22
... *also members of his household, built on the foundation of the apostles and prophets, with Christ Jesus himself as the chief cornerstone. In him the whole building is joined together and rises to become a holy temple in the Lord. And in him you too are being built together to become a dwelling in which God lives by His Spirit.*

Forget all of the foibles of the past and the present and instead think of the possibilities of the future. Forget the church politics, pew fodder, enforced tithing, unspoken anti-Semitism, power structures, ecclesiastical hierarchies, more tea vicar, church steeple appeals, Christian aid, yoga in the vestry, marathon heavy-rock worship, robes, bells, smells, choir boys and all other incidentals on the church landscape and ... instead ... think of:

Being members of Christ's household.
Being part of a holy temple in the Lord.
Being a dwelling in which God lives by his Spirit.

All else pales into insignificance and, if it distracts from this noble purpose, may deflect you from your true function. We are now reminded of the passage that illustrates the shalom of unity that we should all aspire to:

Just as a body, though one, has many parts, but all its many parts form one body, so it is with Christ. For we were all baptized by one Spirit so as to form one body—whether Jews or Gentiles, slave or free—and we were all given the one Spirit to drink. Even so the body is not made up of one part but of many. (1 Corinthians 12:12-14)

One God, one Saviour, one Spirit, one Body. Mark this in your mind, one Body. Not 40,000+ bodies, all working independently, each with its own network of its own bodies, also mostly working independently. *There's too many of us,* you declare, *how on earth can we make up just one body?*

Here's where we are meant to be different from the world. Secular corporations run on acknowledged hierarchies and chains of command and an intertwined complexity of systems, covering finance, sales, marketing, resources, production and so on. This enables the man at the top to control his board, which in turn controls their departments, all the way down the hierarchy to the humble and most expendable employee.

What about the *ekklesia*? The denominational system works in a similar manner to the secular model, that's just how it has evolved, ever since the Kingdom of God was dragged into the world. But is this what is meant to be and can it be any different?

Think of the Body of Christ, as described in the 1 Corinthians passage above. What this doesn't mean is that all members of the Body are living and working in isolation. We are called to be in fellowship with other parts of the Body.

And let us consider how we may spur one another on toward love and good deeds, not giving up meeting together, as some are in the habit of doing, but encouraging one another—and all the more as you see the Day approaching. (Hebrews 10:24-25)

So could the model be of thousands of small gatherings

of believers, not too small as to be ineffective, not too large as to be unwieldly? No hierarchies, just a horizontal line of small fellowships, each consisting of a horizontal line of like-minded believers. And how do these small gatherings communicate with the wider Body stretched throughout the world? *That is surely the 64 million dollar question.*

The worldly Church of the denominations does this through hierarchies and chains of authority that it has copied from the secular business world. How should the *ekklesia* do it?

1. Through horizontal relationships – between the various scattered expressions – the internet has made this easy to do.

2. Through a vertical relationship – *through the Spirit Who connects us all. i.e. supernaturally.*

As long as we cut out the middle man we are fine. It was meant to happen at the Reformation: no more priests and intermediaries, just direct access to God, through the power of the Holy Spirit, in the Name of Jesus. Also, we don't need the 'professional' clergy to authorise our horizontal relationships. If there is control here, then it is usually born out of fear ... of losing control, members, income etc. There shouldn't be any 'barriers of entry' for us to meet up with others in the *ekklesia*, wherever in the world they may be, Free movement, no passports needed.

The Body of Christ is a wonderful thing when unleashed. Every member of the *ekklesia* working together and belonging to each other:

For just as each of us has one body with many members, and these members do not all have the same function, so in Christ we, though many, form one body, and each member belongs to all the others. We have different gifts, according to the grace given to each of us. If your gift is prophesying, then prophesy in accordance with your faith; if it is serving, then serve; if it is teaching, then teach; if it is to encourage, then give encouragement; if it is giving, then give generously; if it is to lead, do it diligently; if it is to show mercy, do it cheerfully. (Romans 12:4-8)

Here's something most of us have said at some point; *but that's not my thing, I don't have the gift of evangelism.* Yes, I've been there and have lived most of my Christian life accordingly. In fact I can't remember the last person that I led into a living faith in Jesus. Well, that's a cop-out because we may not all have been called as evangelists (form), but we are all capable of evangelising (function), as God empowers us accordingly. In fact, as I look through the lists of spiritual gifts in Romans 12, 1 Corinthians 12 and Ephesians 4, there have been times when God has used me many times according to the function, rather than the form. For instance, there have been two recent occasions where Monica and I were used in a pastoral sense, without being pastors. There's a church that considers me as their apostle, because of the impact of the teaching in my books, but that doesn't make me an apostle, in the positional sense. Repeat with the gifts of exhortation, giving, leadership, prophecy, discernment, healing, knowledge and the picture develops of the Body of Christ, equipped for whatever tasks God has for us, with the right tools for the right occasion. It's rather wonderful.

Yet there's an anomaly. Having combed through the three main lists of spiritual gifts, as well as a few other places, I noticed something strange that I had never noticed before. There is no spiritual gift of ... *worship*. For what is seen and promoted as perhaps the most spiritual of disciplines, there is no mention. Strange! Given that, in our culture, worship is most often expressed as sung music, what does the Bible say?

Here are the five main relevant New Testament passages. First the two places where music is part of the narrative:

When they had sung a hymn, they went out to the Mount of Olives. (Matthew 26:30)

About midnight Paul and Silas were praying and singing hymns to God, and the other prisoners were listening to them. (Acts 16:25)

Just a group of people singing hymns, with no sign of a worship leader (or musical instruments). Then there are the instructional verses:

What then shall we say, brothers and sisters? When you come together, each of you has a hymn, or a word of instruction, a revelation, a tongue or an interpretation. Everything must be done so that the church may be built up. (1 Corinthians 14:26)

Speaking to one another with psalms, hymns, and songs from the Spirit. Sing and make music from your heart to the Lord, (Ephesians 5:19)

Let the message of Christ dwell among you richly as you teach and admonish one another with all wisdom through psalms, hymns, and songs from the Spirit, singing to God with gratitude in your hearts. (Colossians 3:16)

That's just about it, in terms of the early Church. They certainly sang hymns, but no sense of led worship. The only time the New Testament speaks of worship, it's in a sense of a function of the heart, not anything specifically to do with music.

"God is spirit, and his worshipers must worship in the Spirit and in truth." (John 4:24)

Worship musicians, though, are in the Bible, in the Old Testament.

The whole assembly bowed in worship, while the musicians played and the trumpets sounded. All this continued until the sacrifice of the burnt offering was completed. (2 Chronicles 29:28)

David and all Israel were celebrating with all their might before the LORD, with castanets, harps, lyres, timbrels, sistrums and cymbals. (2 Samuel 6:5)

David told the leaders of the Levites to appoint their fellow Levites as musicians to make a joyful sound with musical instruments: lyres, harps and cymbals. (1 Chronicles 15:16)

At the dedication of the wall of Jerusalem, the Levites were sought out from where they lived and were brought to Jerusalem to celebrate joyfully the dedication with songs of thanksgiving and with the music of cymbals, harps and lyres. (Nehemiah 12:27)

So, it seems, the Church worship model is taken from the communal celebrations in the Old Testament. This may seem confusing, as many in the Church are convinced that they are *New Testament people* and that the *New has supplanted the Old*. More of this later on.

The Shalom of Unity 13

In my formative years as a young Christian, travelling round, experiencing a variety of Christian expressions, from ultra-charismatic to super-reformed, one thing always puzzled me; *how come God always seemed to adapt to the theology of the congregation?* In reformed churches, He was in the Bible readings, in the high churches He was in the sacraments, in the emergent churches He was in the love expressed between folk and in the charismatic churches He was in the never-ending prophecies, tongues and various manifestations. Each expression would emphasise theirs as the only authentic expression and it seem to make a lie out of Paul's words in Romans 12:5, *in Christ we, though many, form one body, and each member belongs to all the others.*

It was only when I researched such things that the context became clear. It was nothing about God adapting to our needs, it was about man straying from His needs. The reformed churches tended to believe that the spiritual gifts ceased in the 1st Century, hence their reliance solely on the Word. The High churches still held onto the medieval doctrines, influenced by Aristotle, of external rituals being the key to God's heart. The emergent churches were sure that the church must change with the times and promoted a one-dimensional 'God of Love', as if that was the sum-total of His character and attributes. And the charismatics emphasised experience over all, allowing emotions often to cloud the proceedings.

We have made it all about ourselves and we have

brought *ra* into the equation, chaos and division. The antidote is to work towards the true *shalom of unity* and it is worth revisiting the first model of Church. We'll do this by reading 1 Corinthians 12 in its entirety to reboot this whole issue:

Now about the gifts of the Spirit, brothers and sisters, I do not want you to be uninformed. You know that when you were pagans, somehow or other you were influenced and led astray to mute idols. Therefore I want you to know that no one who is speaking by the Spirit of God says, "Jesus be cursed," and no one can say, "Jesus is Lord," except by the Holy Spirit. There are different kinds of gifts, but the same Spirit distributes them. There are different kinds of service, but the same Lord. There are different kinds of working, but in all of them and in everyone it is the same God at work. Now to each one the manifestation of the Spirit is given for the common good. To one there is given through the Spirit a message of wisdom, to another a message of knowledge by means of the same Spirit, to another faith by the same Spirit, to another gifts of healing by that one Spirit, to another miraculous powers, to another prophecy, to another distinguishing between spirits, to another speaking in different kinds of tongues, and to still another the interpretation of tongues. All these are the work of one and the same Spirit, and he distributes them to each one, just as he determines. Just as a body, though one, has many parts, but all its many parts form one body, so it is with Christ. For we were all baptized by one Spirit so as to form one body—whether Jews or Gentiles, slave or free—and we were all given the one Spirit to drink. Even so the body is not made up of one part but of many. Now if the foot should say, "Because I am not a hand, I do not belong to the body," it would not for that reason stop being part of the body. And if the ear should say, "Because I am not an eye, I do not belong to the body," it would not for that reason stop being part of the body. If the whole body were an eye, where would the sense of hearing be? If the whole body were an ear, where would the sense of smell be? But in fact God has placed the parts in the body, every one of them, just as he wanted them to be. If they were all one part, where would the body be? As it is, there are many parts, but one body. The eye cannot say to the hand, "I don't need you!" And the head cannot say to the feet, "I don't need you!" On the contrary, those parts of the body that seem to be weaker are indispensable, and the parts that we think are less honourable we treat with special honour. And the parts that are unpresentable are treated with special modesty, while our presentable parts need no special treatment. But God has put the body together, giving greater honour to the parts that lacked it, so that there should be no division in the body, but that its parts should have equal concern for each other. If one part suffers, every part suffers with it; if one part is honoured, every part rejoices with it. Now you are the body of Christ, and each one of you is a part of it. And God has placed in the church first of all apostles, second prophets, third teachers, then miracles, then gifts of healing, of helping, of guidance, and of different kinds of tongues. Are all apostles? Are all prophets? Are all teachers? Do all work miracles? Do all have gifts of healing? Do all speak in tongues? Do all interpret? Now eagerly desire the greater gifts.

Yes, it's been a big chunk to read, but this is Holy Scripture and far more important than anything I could say! This is a fly on the wall of a 1st Century *ekklesia*. What we mustn't do is to read this and assume that the charismatics are the only ones that have it right. They have the language ... *but not always the application*. We will build on this.

Here it is. All gifts are from the Lord and are for the good of the whole congregation, not the individual. Every believer is open to the possibility of spiritual gifts, whether they are wisdom, knowledge, faith, healing, miracles, prophecy, discernment, tongues or interpretations and it is up to God *who gets what*. All gifts work together and all who exercise them should be treated with equal respect, although some gifts, such as those of apostles, prophets and teachers, are considered the *greater gifts*. Then, of course, as we saw in the previous chapter, are the gifts that God will allow to flow through us, according to the occasion.

This is the ideal, but humans being humans, things can go wrong, as Paul explains a couple of chapters later, in 1 Corinthians 14.

Follow the way of love and eagerly desire gifts of the Spirit, especially prophecy. For anyone who speaks in a tongue does not speak to people but to God. Indeed, no one understands them; they utter mysteries by the Spirit. But the one who prophesies speaks to people for their strengthening, encouraging and comfort. Anyone who speaks in a tongue edifies themselves, but the one who prophesies edifies the church. I would like every one of you to speak in tongues, but I would rather have you prophesy. The one who prophesies is greater than the one who speaks in tongues, unless someone interprets, so that the church may be edified ... What then shall we say, brothers and sisters? When you come together, each of you has a hymn, or a word of instruction, a revelation, a tongue or an interpretation. Everything must be done so that the church may be built up. If anyone speaks in a tongue, two–or at the most three–should speak, one at a time, and someone must interpret. If there is no interpreter, the speaker should keep quiet in the church and speak to himself and to God ... Therefore, my brothers and sisters, be eager to prophesy, and do not forbid speaking in tongues. But everything should be done in a fitting and orderly way.

It is clear that things were not necessarily done in an orderly way and it is clear, from some of the more extreme charismatic expressions that I have visited, a thorough re-reading of the above verses (including the ones missed out) is in order!

Then we look at 2 Timothy 3:16-17

All Scripture is God-breathed and is useful for teaching, rebuking, correcting and training in righteousness, so that the servant of God may be thoroughly equipped for every good work.

This reminds us of the primacy of the Bible, as all Scripture is from God and will equip us for all good work. Again, what we mustn't do is to read this and assume that the reformers are the only ones that have it right. They have the language … *but not always the application.*

We may have the words, but we don't always use them well.

But in your hearts revere Christ as Lord. Always be prepared to give an answer to everyone who asks you to give the reason for the hope that you have. But do this with gentleness and respect, keeping a clear conscience, so that those who speak maliciously against your good behaviour in Christ may be ashamed of their slander. (1 Peter 3:15-16)

Then we have the High Church and their sacraments and rituals and perhaps we feel a little negative towards them, in the light of the Reformation and the accompanying *Sola Scriptura* (Scripture alone), *Sola Fide* (Faith alone), and *Sola Gratia* (Grace alone). But maybe there are a few babies in the bathwater? Some of the sacraments are a reflection of Biblical injunctions:

Therefore go and make disciples of all nations, **baptizing them** *in the name of the Father and of the Son and of the Holy Spirit,* (Matthew 28:19)

For I received from the Lord what I also passed on to you: The Lord Jesus, on the night he was betrayed, took bread, and when he had given thanks, he broke it and said, "This is my body, which is for you; do this in remembrance of me." In the same way, after supper he took the cup, saying, "This cup is the new covenant in my blood; do this, whenever you drink it, in remembrance of me."
For **whenever you eat this bread and drink this cup***, you*

proclaim the Lord's death until he comes. (1 Corinthians 11:23-26)
*If we **confess our sins**, he is faithful and just and will forgive us our sins and purify us from all unrighteousness.* (1 John 1:9)
*Is anyone among you sick? Let them call the elders of the church to pray over them and **anoint them with oil** in the name of the Lord.* (James 5:14)

These all have a place in the *ekklesia*, but not all of them are consistently practised when people come together.

Of course we know that, as with the charismatics and reformers, the High Church people don't always get it right. They have the language ... *but not always the application*, as we can see from the following passage, entitled *when Holy Communion goes wrong* (though this can happen in any Church expression):

So then, when you come together, it is not the Lord's Supper you eat, for when you are eating, some of you go ahead with your own private suppers. As a result, one person remains hungry and another gets drunk. Don't you have homes to eat and drink in? Or do you despise the church of God by humiliating those who have nothing? What shall I say to you? Shall I praise you? Certainly not in this matter! (1 Corinthians 11:20-22)

Then, finally, we have the emergent church, with its accent on love and peace. There's certainly a place for love and peace:

"A new command I give you: Love one another. As I have loved you, so you must love one another. By this everyone will know that you are my disciples, if you love one another." (John 13:34-35)

Sadly, most churches fall down on this one. It's the holy grail, so to speak. If we can really get this one right then surely evangelism would be a piece of cake. Who can fail to be attracted to a group of people who have sincere, demonstrated love for each other?

Of course I can't leave this section without at least some discomfort for the emergent church:

... for I, the LORD your God, am a jealous God, punishing the children for the sin of the parents to the third and fourth generation of those who hate me ... (Exodus 20:5). God is not just about love and peace, there is far more to Him than the emergents dare to imagine.

It is tempting for all of us to defend our own 'tribe' and suggest that all other 'tribes' are lacking in some way. But the fact is that all the expressions covered above had some measure of the truth, it is just rare to find a church that has the lot; a church that functions equally in the Word and the Spirit, that cherishes Biblical ritual and is known for the love that it shows within and without.

So here we have the whole as the greater than its parts. For *ekklesia* to be in shalom, in completeness, there must be full use of spiritual gifts, alongside reverence for the Word, without neglecting the necessary actions (baptism, confession, communion, anointing with oil) and all wrapped up in a love that shows the world that we are truly God's people. And, on top of this, to be a place where every member of that congregation is aware of their *function* in the Body of Christ and is exercising this function. This is the s*halom of unity* and our fellowships must operate in a way that allows all aspects to function *according to the Maker's instructions.*

PART FOUR
The Shalom of Oneness

Shabbat, shalom?   14

So what's this with the Church? For a movement birthed by Jews, spread by Jews and informed by their writings and practices, there is a massive disconnect between those times and today. Any objective analysis can only come to one conclusion, the Church has deliberately cut itself off from its roots and this begs us to ask why this should be. Another question could also be to wonder why those natural roots were replaced by harmful ideas and practices taken from cultures and movements in direct opposition to the stated aims of the Church of Jesus Christ?

In the early days, the key points of contention were regarding two things. Firstly the day of the week God expressly set aside for rest, the *Sabbath* (***Shabbat***). And secondly the timing of the celebration of Jesus' resurrection at *Passover* (***Pesach***) time. Arguably the two most important days on God's calendar, adding a sinister feel to the situation! In both cases we need to look at the cause of the problem and the effect that it has on all parties.

First the Sabbath. Its form is just that it's a day of the week, yet, Biblically, it's a *specific* day of the week, the seventh day aka Saturday (the day we commemorate the Roman god and planet Saturn), with a specific function, *as a day of rest*. According to the Bible it is the seventh day of the week, but not according to the secular International standard (ISO 8601), since 1988, which deems Saturday the sixth day. All through the Bible the Sabbath retains its place as the seventh day, including the New Testament, with both Jesus and Paul acknowledging it so. Yet, in the Church today, *Sunday* is now deemed to be the Sabbath, or at least the day people 'do Church'. Why the change, if the Bible doesn't command it?

<controversial statement alert>
Actually I don't think it is a change.

It's not that the Church has changed the Sabbath, *in its original meaning as a day of rest*, from a Saturday to a Sunday, it's just that the Church has decided that it was only going to meet up once a week and that day should be a Sunday, the day of Jesus' resurrection. What we should instead be asking is **why the Church stopped celebrating the Saturday Sabbath** *as a day of rest* **and why it decided that God only requires our presence on one day a week, the Sunday?**

To answer these questions, we need to review the early history of the Church. This is tricky as there's little historical data available for the period between the closing of the Book of Acts and the rise of the early Church Fathers, such as Justin Martyr. We know that the Jewish Christians, known as Nazarenes, fled to Pella in the east, where they existed until the Fourth Century, tenaciously holding on to Jewish observances and Torah teaching, keeping the Saturday Sabbath and the dates of Passover according to Jewish tradition.

Meanwhile the Gentile Church was scattered throughout the Roman Empire and not having a good time of it, with sporadic persecutions. Until Jerusalem was destroyed in AD 135, Christianity was considered as a sect of the Jews and so Sabbath observance was the norm. But now that the Jews were *persona non grata*, the Christians, in order to blend in and stay out of trouble, began to adopt a Sunday "Sabbath", in line with

Mithraism, the accepted religion of the Roman Empire. These were the plain facts, expedience rather than any study of the New Testament that may have convinced them that *God had changed His mind about the Sabbath.* To remind us, here's His first (and final) say on the matter, the fourth commandment:

"Remember the Sabbath day by keeping it holy. Six days you shall labour and do all your work, but the seventh day is a sabbath to the LORD your God. On it you shall not do any work, neither you, nor your son or daughter, nor your male or female servant, nor your animals, nor any foreigner residing in your towns. For in six days the LORD made the heavens and the earth, the sea, and all that is in them, but he rested on the seventh day. Therefore the LORD blessed the Sabbath day and made it holy." (Exodus 20:8-11)

This is an awkward and embarrassing passage for many Christians, who insist that, although Jesus has *affirmed* the other nine commandments, he, for some reason, remained silent on this one. Yet Jesus was very vocal on those who misunderstood the meaning of the Sabbath, with what surely must be his last word on the subject:

Then he said to them, "The Sabbath was made for man, not man for the Sabbath. So the Son of Man is Lord even of the Sabbath." (Mark 2:27-28)

If Jesus was Lord even of the Sabbath, doesn't that imply that it still had relevance, just like everything else Jesus was Lord over, otherwise he would have added such words as, *and anyway it has no meaning for you now that I am here?*

So, Biblically, there is nothing explicitly that suggests that God has done away with the Sabbath, so the *function* remains the same, even if the *form* may change. What do I mean by that? As we said earlier, the function of the

Sabbath is *to provide a time of rest*:

By the seventh day God had finished the work he had been doing; so on the seventh day he rested from all his work. Then God blessed the seventh day and made it holy, because on it he rested from all the work of creating that he had done (Genesis 2:2-3)

Even Christians, whether Jew or Gentile, are reminded of the function of the Sabbath:

There remains, then, a Sabbath-rest for the people of God; for anyone who enters God's rest also rests from their works, just as God did from his. Let us, therefore, make every effort to enter that rest, so that no one will perish by following their example of disobedience. (Hebrews 4:9-11)

The function remains the same, but what about the *form*? This is where there is contention. For Christians there seem to be three possibilities:

1. The Sabbath rest is for an arbitrary day, given that in the Genesis Creation account, there is no way of knowing whether the First day of Creation was actually a Sunday, by our reckoning and, consequently, whether the Sabbath is on a Saturday, by our reckoning. As God has yet to make His covenants with Abraham and Moses, it is more important to dwell on the *function*, the day of rest, rather than wondering what actual day is being referred to.

2. The Sabbath rest is for the seventh day of the week, as described within the Ten Commandments. As the Ten Commandments are part of God's covenant with Moses, we can assume that the actual day, the seventh day of the week had been fixed into the Hebrew calendar (though, of course, it wouldn't have been called Saturday, as the pagan god Saturn hadn't yet been invented!)

3. Rather than speaking of a single 24 hour period, the "Sabbath rest" is the experience of living in the light of the Gospel, in God's Kingdom.

Rather than critiquing each, we should move forwards in the light of the recommended attitude of Romans 14:

One person considers one day more sacred than another; another considers every day alike. Each of them should be fully convinced in their own mind. Whoever regards one day as special does so to the Lord ...You, then, why do you judge your brother or sister? Or why do you treat them with contempt? For we will all stand before God's judgment seat. It is written: "'As surely as I live,' says the Lord, 'every knee will bow before me; every tongue will acknowledge God.'" So then, each of us will give an account of ourselves to God. Therefore let us stop passing judgment on one another. Instead, make up your mind not to put any stumbling block or obstacle in the way of a brother or sister. (verses 5-6, 10-13)

Let's not judge each other, yet, also, let us not forget that God commands us to rest, however we may interpret this. In the light of this let us return to the first question posed earlier:

Why did the Church stop celebrating the Saturday Sabbath *as a day of rest?*

The answer is given by the official proclamation of Emperor Constantine, the man who created the concept of *Christendom*, with Christianity as the official religion of the Roman Empire. Here's his first proclamation regarding the change of Sabbath, in AD 321:

"On the venerable Day of the Sun let the magistrates and people residing in cities rest, and let all workshops be closed."

This was made a lot more official in AD 364, with the proclamation (Canon 29) of the Council of Laodicea:

"Christians shall not Judaize and be idle on Saturday but shall work on that day; but the Lord's day they shall especially honour, and, as being Christians, shall, if possible, do no work on that day. If, however, they are found Judaizing, they shall be shut out from Christ."

What do we conclude from this? Firstly, that the instigation of the change of the "Sabbath" was political and borne out of the "Christian" anti-Semitism that was endemic to "Christendom" (For more on this, read my book **Outcast Nation**).

Secondly, that the initial intention was to emulate the mechanism of the Sabbath through enforcement. If this is no different to what the Jewish people are urged to do on a Sabbath, then we are simply moving the Sabbath from Saturday to Sunday. I would suggest that there is something different going on here, culminating in an artificial construct, not prompted by Scripture, but rather by man.

The Church of Constantine was one born out of political expediency. After all, if Christianity was going to be the official religion of the Roman Empire, then it would effectively be the tool of the Roman Empire, in order to be able to rule the people effectively. And what better way was there to unify the Empire than to give them a set of ideas to believe in? The trouble is that Christianity itself wasn't unified, so his first task was to firm up a unified set of beliefs and then give firm instructions how these beliefs should be followed. All this was done at the council of Nicaea and out of this came the newly constructed churches and cathedrals (that we explored in an earlier chapter), with a prescribed day, the Sunday – the existing pagan day for communal worship – to practice their "Christianity".

And this answers the second question posed earlier. **Why was it decided that God only requires our presence on one day a week, the Sunday?**

If this new "religion" of Christianity was to be an effective tool for the State, then it needed to realise that it had to abide by the State's rules. It suited Constantine and those who followed to declare to the people that their only religious obligations were to attend Church on a Sunday and try to abstain from work that day. Thus was born the Sunday "Sabbath", a day that has retained this prescribed function right up to today. This is a day when many Christians, unconsciously following the dualistic mindset of Plato, grant a few hours of their time to "spiritual matters" and retain the rest of their time for their own purposes. And, of course, the "day of rest" motif has gradually been eaten away by creeping secularisation, with High Streets usually busier and noisier on a Sunday than any other day of the week!

And on a curious but telling note, the actual word *Shabbat* (Sabbath) has the three letter Hebrew root of *Shin – Bet – Tav*. Although the popular translation of this is as "rest", a secondary translation focusses on the letters themselves and notices their similarity to the Hebrew word for the number seven, *Sheba, Shin – Bet – Ayin*. This builds up a very strong case for this holy day being celebrated on the *seventh* day, highlighted by its very name. In this way, the idea of a Shabbat being celebrated on the *first* day of the week, makes little sense.

So what can we do, those of us who feel that the seventh day Sabbath has never been rescinded, Biblically speaking?

Let us revisit Genesis 2:

By the seventh day God had finished the work he had been doing; so on the seventh day he rested from all his work. Then God blessed the seventh day and made it holy, because on it he rested from all the work of creating that he had done. (Genesis 2:2-3)

These verses are unique in that they contain the first appearance of the word *Kadosh, holy*. According to Abraham Heschel, in his book "The Sabbath" (p. 9, 10):

"There is no reference in the record of creation to any

object in space that would be endowed with the quality of holiness. This is a radical departure from accustomed religious thinking. The mythical mind would expect that, after heaven and earth have been established, God would create a holy place – a holy mountain or a holy spring – whereupon a sanctuary is to be established. Yet it seems as if to the Bible it is *holiness in time*, the Sabbath, which comes first ... The meaning of the Sabbath is to celebrate time rather than space. Six days a week we live under the tyranny of things of space; on the Sabbath we try to become attuned to *holiness in time*. It is a day on which we are called upon to share in what is eternal in time, to turn from the results of creation to the mystery of creation; from the world of creation to the creation of the world."

There is undoubtedly something special about the Sabbath in Jewish thinking. Sages throughout the ages have eulogised this day to the extent of almost deifying it. Here are some examples:

"It is a day for the soul, not of the body. It is the sweetness of souls, the delight of spirits, and the bliss of souls, to be blissful with the love and awe of the Blessed One." (Rabbi Shalom Noach Berezovsky)

"... through a sincere attempt to honour it and enjoy it for the sake of heaven, the Jew earns God's blessing that the Sabbath become holy and radiate its aura into every aspect of his life". (Rabbi Nosson Scherman)

"The Sabbath is the presence of God in the world, open to the soul of man". (Rabbi Abraham Heschel)

There are literally thousands more similar quotations by Rabbis through the ages. I was curious whether there was an equivalent trove of quotations by Christian writers and thinkers, regarding the *Sunday Sabbath*. I found none, though I didn't look very hard. To be honest, if such a collection existed then it wouldn't have been hard to find it.

So what does that tell us? It points to a reverence of the Sabbath as a day in its own right, a holy day instituted by God, backed up by Holy Scripture. This is the Jewish position, but it is not the majority Christian position. There is nothing intrinsically holy about the Sunday Sabbath in the sense of it being divinely appointed, it is simply a political appointment, with the tenuous association with the day of Christ's resurrection, rather than any divine command that it be a "day of rest". The Saturday Sabbath is a Biblical imperative. The Sunday Sabbath is a marriage of convenience.

What are Gentile Christians to do? It is really a matter of personal conscience, guided by those verses in Romans 14 about not placing stumbling blocks in front of others. Whatever you decide to do, *it doesn't mean that everyone else is wrong, unbiblical, to be condemned.* If you feel God is directing you towards a Saturday Sabbath, it should be in the attitude of personal guidance rather than a universal rule, although the concept of a day of rest is thoroughly Biblical. Yet if you are to be consistent with Scripture and with the activities of the Church in Acts, then the Sabbath is not simply a day when we conduct a church service, but rather a time of restorative rest with God and family. A Hebraic attitude would be to celebrate Sabbath in whichever way is right for your particular circumstance and where you are certain God is leading you, which may not be where God is leading others. If you take the Greek attitude of transforming your particular experience into some sort of doctrine or ritual, then you will slip into a judgemental attitude about others who 'just don't get it'! This is not a righteous path and would only serve to feed those 'on the outside' who are suspicious about the motives of those who keep the Sabbath, reinforcing the view that they are 'judaizers'.

If your conscience directs you to meeting with God on a Sunday (i.e. the traditional model), you must be aware of the historical origin of this custom, as described earlier. The danger is to fall into the trap of dualism, considering that a few hours of 'God time' is sufficient to satisfy your 'spiritual needs' and is the only obligation you need to make to your Maker and Redeemer. Yes, by all means meet with God in church on a Sunday, but don't neglect Him the rest of the week!

There is a danger concerning Gentile Christians and the Saturday Sabbath. If we revisit those eulogies by the rabbis, there's a danger that we too can start to consider this holy day in ways that are unbiblical. Just with those three examples given, which are representative of the Jewish orthodox community, Sabbath is "a day for the soul and not the body, that it radiates its aura into all aspects of life and that it represents God's presence in the world."

Can you see the implications? The Rabbis may have had a certain spirituality but one thing they didn't have: the fulness of the Holy Spirit living in their hearts as a result of their submission to Jesus their Messiah. These eulogies can be seen as a substitute for Messiah. Perhaps this is why the writer of the Hebrew wrote the following?

There remains, then, a Sabbath-rest for the people of God; for anyone who enters God's rest also rests from their works, just as God did from his. Let us, therefore, make every effort to enter that rest, so that no one will perish by following their example of disobedience. (Hebrews 4:9-11)

This could be a reminder that the Sabbath, rather than being a substitute for Jesus, is an attribute of the rest that our Messiah has brought to us. But does this mean that the Sabbath Day is no longer valid for us? As I said earlier, it really is a matter of personal leading from the Lord. On a personal note, the Lord has given me a passage that is very pertinent to the Foundations ministry that He has called me into:

Your people will rebuild the ancient ruins and will raise up the age-old foundations; you will be called Repairer of Broken Walls, Restorer of Streets with Dwellings. (Isaiah 58:12)

Yet ... the very next verses:

"If you keep your feet from breaking the Sabbath and from doing as you please on my holy day, if you call the Sabbath a delight and the LORD's holy day honourable, and if you honour it by not going your own way and not doing as you please or speaking idle words, then you will find your joy in the LORD, and I will cause you to ride in triumph on the heights of the land and to feast on the inheritance of your father Jacob." For the mouth of the LORD has spoken. (Isaiah 58:13-14)

This is some promise! As I have stressed before, the Lord has different callings and functions for us all. It may seem that I am currently balancing on the fence regarding Sabbath, but, in all honesty, Monica and I are still on a journey with this issue and we want to be true to ourselves in any decision we make, as there will be no going back. One thing is certain, *you'll know when we know.*

Passover or pass me by?

15

Most of us celebrate the day of our birth. Some of us even have the day of our death celebrated, although we are not around to bask in all the attention! Although there are Biblical examples of folk returning after death, only one person has had his return from death still celebrated over 2,000 years afterwards. You'd think this unique, significant occasion would have its day sealed in stone, permanently inscribed in the records of human history. You'd be wrong.

The fact that the date of Jesus' resurrection is contested and used divisively ironically demonstrates its importance, due to the propensity of Christians to royally mess the important things up!

After the Sabbath, at dawn on the first day of the week, Mary Magdalene and the other Mary went to look at the tomb. (Matthew 28:1)

The early Church acknowledged the historical setting for this event and celebrated it based on the day of the Passover meal, Nisan 14th in the Hebrew calendar, considered to be the day of the crucifixion, although the correct day would more probably have been Nisan 15th. So we already have confusion. The practice of celebrating these events on Nisan 14th even had a name, *Quartodecimanism*, just one of the many -isms churned out by the Greek-influenced Church and simply being the Latin phrase for "the fourteeners".

Jewish Christians at this time had a dilemma. Should they celebrate Passover in the traditional sense with other

Jews, or a 'Passover-in-the-light-of-Jesus' among themselves? In 175 AD, Melito of Sardis, (said to be fifth in line in terms of apostolic succession, starting with the apostle John), facilitated the latter by creating the first Passover Haggadah (Passover order of service), *Peri Pascha*, that took Jesus into account. It starts by recounting the Exodus story from Exodus 12, but splices in Jesus' story, prompted by 1 Corinthians 5:7-8:

For Christ, our Passover lamb, has been sacrificed. Therefore let us keep the Festival, not with the old bread leavened with malice and wickedness, but with the unleavened bread of sincerity and truth.

In the *Peri Pasch*a, Melito compares Jesus' victory over death with Moses' victory over Pharaoh. He also identifies the broken Matzah (unleavened bread) with the broken body of Jesus and also develops the theme of the *afikomen*, the bread that is hidden away and brought back near the end of the service. He speaks of this in the context of Jesus' return, even using a Greek term, *aphikomenos*, to refer to this. Surely this was a worthy exercise, cementing the Christian faith into the practices of the Jewish events that underpinned it? Worthy it may have been, but the new Church leaders thought otherwise.

At the end of the 2nd Century, Pope Victor I tried to excommunicate those who were using these dates, in order to maintain some kind of unity in the Church. He failed. The fact is that by this time many were favouring the closest Sunday to the date, in order to match up with the Gospel record, if not the *actual* date.

The growing anti-Jewish sentiment in the Church reached a new level when the Emperor Constantine declared Christianity as the State religion of the Roman Empire. On the issue of the dating of Resurrection Day he was adamant, but he certainly wasn't Prince Charming (obscure 1980s pop music reference, look it up). He made his position clear in a letter written after the Council of Nicaea in 325AD. Here is the letter in full, with pertinent content in bold:

*"At this meeting the question concerning the most holy day of Easter was discussed, and it was resolved by the united judgment of all present, that this feast ought to be kept by all and in every place on one and the same day. For what can be more becoming or honourable to us than that this feast from which we date our hopes of immortality, should be observed unfailingly by all alike, according to one ascertained order and arrangement? And first of all, it appeared an unworthy thing that in the celebration of this most holy feast we should follow the practice of **the Jews, who have impiously defiled their hands with enormous sin, and are, therefore, deservedly afflicted with blindness of soul.** For we have it in our power, if we abandon their custom, to prolong the due observance of this ordinance to future ages, by a truer order, which we have preserved from the very day of the passion until the present time. **Let us then have nothing in common with the detestable Jewish crowd;** for we have received from our Saviour a different way. A course at once legitimate and honourable lies open to our most holy religion. Beloved brethren, let us with one consent adopt this course, and withdraw ourselves from all participation in their baseness. For their boast is absurd indeed, that it is not in our power without instruction from them to observe these things. For how should they be capable of forming a sound judgment, who, **since their parricidal guilt in slaying their Lord, have been subject to the direction, not of reason, but of ungoverned passion, and are swayed by every impulse of the mad spirit that is in them?** Hence it is that on this point as well as others they have no perception of the truth, so that, being altogether ignorant of the true adjustment of this question, they sometimes celebrate Easter twice in the same year. Why then should we follow those who are confessedly in grievous error?*

Surely we shall never consent to keep this feast a second time in the same year. But supposing these reasons were not of sufficient weight, still it would be incumbent on your Sagacities to strive and pray continually that the purity of your souls may not seem in anything to be sullied by fellowship with the customs of these most wicked men. We must consider, too, that a discordant judgment in a case of such importance, and respecting such religious festival, is wrong. For our Saviour has left us one feast in commemoration of the day of our deliverance, I mean the day of his most holy passion; and he has willed that his Catholic Church should be one, the members of which, however scattered in many and diverse places, are yet cherished by one pervading spirit, that is, by the will of God. And let your Holinesses' sagacity reflect how grievous and scandalous it is that on the self-same days some should be engaged in fasting, others in festive enjoyment; and again, that after the days of Easter some should be present at banquets and amusements, while others are fulfilling the appointed fasts. It is, then, plainly the will of Divine Providence (as I suppose you all clearly see), that this usage should receive fitting correction, and be reduced to one uniform rule."

As a politician, he achieved his objectives under the pretence of "unity", but as a Christian afflicted with the virus of anti-Semitism he couldn't resist some very nasty digs towards the Jewish people. So Passover was no more in Christendom, replaced by *Easter*, named after an old English goddess called *Eostre*, who already happened to have a feast in her honour at that time of the year. In terms of the timing of Easter, the initial binding rules were its total independence from the Jewish calendar (and the *actual* date of the festival) and the need for universal acceptance in the name of Church unity. Nowadays in the West, Easter falls on the first Sunday after the full moon after the March equinox.

What has really happened, as with the Sabbath

controversy, is that a Biblical event has been stripped from its context and applied according to the whims of the rulers of the established Church. God just didn't have a say in it. Nobody asked Him what He thought of it or probably even informed Him of their decision once it had been made. Just one of many symptoms of a Church that has abandoned the original model of a God-centred enterprise and has created a new model that puts Man and his needs dead centre.

In the next chapter we return to the original model, the Biblical passage that ought to have provided a manifesto for a healthy and balanced Church, but, instead seems to have been one of the most ignored or misunderstood mysteries in Pauls writings.

The Shalom of Oneness 16

Let's cut straight to the chase and read Paul's (and God's) blueprint for the model of a Church that integrates the people who are near (the Jews) and the people who are far away (the Gentiles).

Therefore, remember that formerly you who are Gentiles by birth and called "uncircumcised" by those who call themselves "the circumcision" (which is done in the body by human hands) – remember that at that time you were separate from Christ, excluded from citizenship in Israel and foreigners to the covenants of the promise, without hope and without God in the world. But now in Christ Jesus you who once were far away have been brought near by the blood of Christ. For he himself is our peace, who has made the two groups one and has destroyed the barrier, the dividing wall of hostility, by setting aside in his flesh the law with its commands and regulations. His purpose was to create in himself one new humanity out of the two, thus making peace, and in one body to reconcile both of them to God through the cross, by which he put to death their hostility. He came and preached peace to you who were far away and peace to those who were near. For through him we both have access to the Father by one Spirit. (Ephesians 2:11-18)

Before we feed from the truth within these words, it's worth considering context, particularly as it begins with "Therefore ...", implying a set-up and followed by "Consequently ...", implying ... consequences. So, first the set-up:

He reminds us of God's perspective, as the whole initiative is His, through His grace. So we read the preceding verses from His perspective, not ours:

As for you, you were dead in your transgressions and sins, in which you used to live when you followed the ways of this world and of the ruler of the kingdom of the air, the spirit who is now at work in those who are disobedient. All of us also lived among them at one time, gratifying the cravings of our flesh and following its desires and thoughts. Like the rest, we were by nature deserving of wrath. But because of his great love for us, God, who is rich in mercy, made us alive with Christ even when we were dead in transgressions–it is by grace you have been saved. And God raised us up with Christ and seated us with him in the heavenly realms in Christ Jesus, in order that in the coming ages he might show the incomparable riches of his grace, expressed in his kindness to us in Christ Jesus. For it is by grace you have been saved, through faith–and this is not from yourselves, it is the gift of God– not by works, so that no one can boast. For we are God's handiwork, created in Christ Jesus to do good works, which God prepared in advance for us to do. (Ephesians 2:1-10)

We are the products of God's grace, not the instigators. We are saved as a free gift from God but, despite what some in the Church teach, it is not totally one-sided, *for we have responsibilities too*. We have been created to *do good works*. And, as has already been discussed in the Shalom of Unity, these functions have been individually assigned to us from God Himself. We're not just to hang around in smug expectation of a glorious future.

Paul then reminds Gentiles how far they have come, as the far away people, now brought near by the blood of Christ. Such grace has been bestowed on them, perhaps far more than the Jews, the people who were already near, who already had the covenants and the promises. There is one thing they must now take very seriously. It comes in verses 14 to 18:

For he himself is our peace, who has made the two groups one and has destroyed the barrier, the dividing wall of hostility, by setting aside in his flesh the law with its commands and regulations. His purpose was to create in himself one new humanity out of the two, thus making peace, and in one body to reconcile both of them to God through the cross, by which he put to death their hostility. He came and preached peace to you who were far away and peace to those who were near. For through him we both have access to the Father by one Spirit.

There is one main objective expressed, that of peace, shalom, the *shalom of oneness*, where the near people and the far away people become one people, One New Humanity, or *One New Man*, as it is more universally expressed. This is no ordinary shalom, it has been instigated by Jesus himself, who, through his sacrifice on the cross has totally done away with the sacrificial system, the barrier that differentiated the two people. By doing so, they are now one people, the near people and the far people now together becoming *the people of the one Spirit*.

Hostility between the groups has been put to death and peace now reigns. *Does it really?*

Perhaps we should remind the Gentiles how they have utterly failed mostly to follow this narrative, with centuries of hostility towards the Jewish people, thus rendering these verses a nonsense in their application of them. It is bad enough that "Christians" have relentlessly persecuted the Jewish people for centuries, but there is still hostility towards Jews who have accepted Christ and *now have access to the Father by the same Spirit*. And it all started, as we saw in the preceding two chapters, with the Gentile Church stripping away the Jewish roots of the faith, starting with the Sabbath and Passover. *One New Man* was cut off in its prime and a lop-sided Church has reigned ever since.

So we have read what should have happened and, in

the following verses, we read what would have been the consequences:

Consequently, you are no longer foreigners and strangers, but fellow citizens with God's people and also members of his household, built on the foundation of the apostles and prophets, with Christ Jesus himself as the chief cornerstone. In him the whole building is joined together and rises to become a holy temple in the Lord. And in him you too are being built together to become a dwelling in which God lives by his Spirit. (Ephesians 2:19-22)

We must remember that Paul is still talking to the Gentiles here and reminding them of the immense privilege they have been granted by being added to God's people. We are reminded of the Olive Tree picture in Romans 11:

If some of the branches have been broken off, and you, though a wild olive shoot, have been grafted in among the others and now share in the nourishing sap from the olive root, do not consider yourself to be superior to those other branches. If you do, consider this: You do not support the root, but the root supports you. (Romans 11:17-18)

Oh how Paul would have grieved if he had known how those in-grafted branches felt themselves so superior to the natural branches that *the holy temple in the Lord,* although supported by impressive Greek columns, would be sinking through lack of foundations and will eventually collapse unless things start to change. Doesn't Paul remind them, in Romans 11:20, *do not be arrogant, but tremble!?*

God is infinitely patient. He has to be, considering the actions of the Gentile Church in the last nineteen centuries towards the Jewish people (and just about everyone else too). If ancient Israel can be exiled through idolatry and disobedience, how merciful God has been to the established Church for a catalogue of major sins and travesties that, by comparison, make the ancient Jews seem no more than naughty schoolboys.

Read that final Ephesians passage again. Isn't the holy temple in the Lord meant to be one built *together*, Jew and Gentile? If our current Church is not built together – Jew and Gentile – *how then can it honestly be a dwelling in which God lives by His Spirit?* If you re-read the whole chapter you realise that Paul places the initiative at the feet of the Gentiles. He is almost saying, *hey you are the new kids on the block, let's see how you play nicely with the local kids.* Well, they didn't make a good job of it, did they?

But what of the Jews? Now that there is a growing Jewish component to the Body of Christ, perhaps things can change for the better? Something has to change. Let's dream a bit. What would our One New Man Church look like, this holy temple in the Lord, if the passage in Ephesians had actually been followed? I'm not sure but I am quite certain that it wouldn't have looked like any fellowship that I have visited claiming to be 'One New Man'. Yes, this may seem to be judgemental of me, but, to be honest, if we are going to base a ministry on a passage of Scripture then the very least we should do is … *base the ministry on the passage of Scripture*. Here are some questions that need to be asked regarding the Shalom of Oneness that we need to see implemented in such ministries:

- How Jewish are they? How many of their practices are taken from post-Biblical rabbinic traditions?
- How Gentile are they? How many Gentile practices are rejected or overlooked?
- Are they always places where Jews are Jews and Gentiles are Gentiles?
- Are they places that actively promote peace between Jew and Gentile?

This is simply an observation, not a condemnation. These fellowships are as valid as any other, as long as they are initiated by God and run according to Biblical principles. The question that I really want to pose for further thought is this:
Could there be a better way?
The rest of this section will explore this question further and may hopefully prompt some considered thought. I believe that we are at the *beginning* of a wonderful journey. Here is my premise. What can we learn from the Jewish experience over the centuries? We know what Gentiles have brought to the table, so to speak, good and bad, because we see this in the Church as it exists today. But the Jews, forced to live a precarious existence thanks to the Gentile Church, have survived bloodied but intact. And they have a story to tell. I am going to attempt to analyse the *Jewish experience*, explore what the One New Man Church might have looked like, and still could look like, if your Christian forbears hadn't made that tragic decision to abandon the Jewish roots of their faith.

Here's a thought to whet your appetite. First, let's consider that well-known verse from Romans 11 about the Jewish people:

Again I ask: Did they stumble so as to fall beyond recovery? Not at all! Rather, because of their transgression, salvation has come to the Gentiles to make Israel envious. But if their transgression means riches for the world, and their loss means riches for the Gentiles, how much greater riches will their full inclusion bring! (Romans 11:11-12)

Now let's turn it on its head and rephrase it. This time, imagine the Gentile Church being the subject of the passage:

Again I ask: Did they stumble so as to fall beyond recovery? Not at all! Rather, because of their transgression, salvation is now

THE SHALOM OF ONENESS

coming back to the Jews to make the Church envious. And how much greater riches are the Jews bringing through the restoration of the Hebraic roots of the faith, lost for centuries!

And what are these *greater riches?* Well, we have already seen two of them, the gifts of the Sabbath and the Passover Seder service. They are both spoken of in Leviticus 23, introduced by the following:

The LORD said to Moses, "Speak to the Israelites and say to them: 'These are my appointed festivals, the appointed festivals of the LORD, which you are to proclaim as sacred assemblies. (Leviticus 23:1-2)

Appointed festivals, appointed times, *Moedim* in Hebrew. At no other time are people of God instructed to proclaim sacred assemblies, so you get a sense of how important *Shabbat* (Sabbath), *Pesach* (Passover) and the rest of the Biblical feasts, particularly *Shavuot* (Pentecost) and *Succoth* (Tabernacles) are to God. If they are important for Him then ....

Simcha   17

In Romans 11 it speaks of the effect on the Church, when the Jews finally return home, as 'life from the dead'. I believe I witnessed certainly a significant aspect of this, having just returned from witnessing the first hour or so of a Sabbath 'service' at the Western Wall in Jerusalem.

It is tempting and perhaps a bit inappropriate to compare this to a typical Christian service, but I will do it anyway, because I'm that awkward! For a start there is no single service, no leaders and no order of service, just spontaneous expression taken from a variety of cultures and customs, but all different ways of expressing worship (though one wonders whether they are truly worshipping God or the Sabbath itself). And it's a major undertaking for many of them just to get there and one assumes that the old babushkas would have had to start their journey mid-afternoon in order to navigate the hundreds of stone steps between the Jewish quarter and the Western Wall plaza. I suspect that the weekly sacrifice is well worth it.

It is a riotous mess and so incredibly moving, when you observe the ebb and flow, of different groups coming to the fore with their singing and dancing, In the time I was there these groups varied from ebullient teenage boys (curiously all dressed in free-flowing white shirt and black trousers) exhibiting dance moves from the Mr Bean school of choreography, but no-one cared as joy rather than 'coolness' was the key driver. Then there were the older orthodox males with swinging *tallit* and flying *kippahs* as they moved as energetically as their old bones could manage. Then there were mixed groups, dragging in stragglers who ventured too close. While this was happening the serious Hasidim with the furry hats were hogging the front row by the wall, oblivious to all but their own individual swaying, as they 'davenned'.

Meanwhile old *schnorrers* (beggars) in religious garb worked the crowd with jangling coins in their cupped hands and young men were accosting anyone who looked vaguely Jewish to don the *tefillin* as an act of obedience. I declined when asked, explaining that God had a different task for me and we all must do whatever is our calling. He shrugged his shoulders and moved on and I must admit there is something quite reverent and touching when you see someone, particularly young men, with serious expressions as they are helped through this complex and cumbersome ritual. It's all so counter-cultural when you think of what other young men of the same age are up to in the world at large.

In the large plaza to the back, there were numerous groups of young people, all dressed to the nines *appropriately* and just talking, singing, hugging and dancing. Not anything I've remotely witnessed outside Faces nightclub in Ilford on a Friday night! Then there was the reverence for where they were, with kippahs mandatory and the fact that, when leaving, one did so walking backwards, at least for the first few steps, otherwise disorder would ensue. This may all seem so hyped-up and sentimental but I'm really not that sort of person (ask Monica). But it so touched me, there was something very clean and holy about it. You really had to be there. Most of all I shed some tears for this, the remnant of centuries of missed opportunities to meet their Jewish Messiah, mostly through the actions of 'Christendom', a counterfeit Church, but also still by sincere Christians who are sincerely wrong and should know better. My final thought was this, if what I experienced here is the response to the bringing in of the Sabbath, think how it will be when they celebrate the *Lord* of the Sabbath!

Then I thought of the Church (I did promise that I would do a comparison). To the average punter visiting the Old City of Jerusalem, one experiences Judaism at the Western Wall and Christianity at the Church of the Holy Sepulchre, supposedly housing both the site of the Crucifixion and the (empty) tomb of Christ. It is apt if we wish to compare the best of one religion, with the worst of the other. Here's what I mean …

You enter through a huge open doorway flanked by Greek columns into a darkened space swarming with humanity, of the tourist persuasion. Once inside the smell of incense hits you, masking the faint whiff of sweat, churned out by the sheer volume of underarm factories. You are faced by a huge cracked stone mounted on a platform and accessible for all. This is supposedly the spot where Jesus' body was prepared for burial. There was a queue of pilgrims eager to take their place kneeling by the stone, kissing it, even rubbing it with wool or cloth. The place was barely lit up, most lamps were unlit and austere paintings of haloed saints are scattered throughout the sprawling building. Black robed priests carrying bunches of candles were ever-vigilant particularly concerning anyone jumping the enormous queue, presumably leading to the 'burial place' within an ornate grotto. *Why visit a place where He isn't?*

I wandered around and there were some interesting nooks and crannies. One contained an office where a grey-bearded (high?) priest was sitting behind a desk speaking on the phone, a huge bowl of sweeties in front of him.

Another contained detritus, stones and building materials for a work in progress. One was a well-lit and tastefully decorated prayer room ... with only four people in attendance! This was significant and re-enforced the reality that this building symbolised empty religion rather than a living faith.

Yes it was an extreme example, but tourists will clearly see the difference between the two religious expressions, barely a few hundred metres apart. One, in the open and lit up from the starry sky above evoked broad, vivid strokes on the canvas of life, drawn with colour and vibrancy, the other, in a dark austere building spoke of darkness and superstition and emptiness and going through the motions of religiosity.

Regarding that Shabbat crowd at the Western Wall, if I were to summarise in one word what was going on around me, that word would be *joy*. Was I getting carried away here, after all, doesn't one need to know the Messiah to experience real joy or is this just Christian wishful thinking? Can there be real joy when there's a messiah-shaped hole in their hearts? Apparently yes, because no other word seemed to be adequate for the singing, dancing, cheerfulness and benign fellowship that reverberated around that place. If joy is what it is, then we need to know exactly what it is and then pose the very real question of why we see little of it in our churches? Is it because the Christian life sucks it out of us?

Rather than consult a dictionary we can do better by looking at how Jesus used the word and then arrive at a relevant definition. Here are some meaty verses to get us thinking:

But the angel said to them, *"Do not be afraid. I bring you good news that will cause great joy for all the people.* (Luke 2:10)

"Rejoice in that day and leap for joy, because great is your

reward in heaven. For that is how their ancestors treated the prophets. (Luke 6:23)

At that time Jesus, full of joy through the Holy Spirit, said, "I praise you, Father, Lord of heaven and earth, because you have hidden these things from the wise and learned, and revealed them to little children. Yes, Father, for this is what you were pleased to do. (Luke 10:21)

I have told you this so that my joy may be in you and that your joy may be complete. (John 15:11)

Joy in these circumstances came about through hearing the gospel and realising its implications, through having the Holy Spirit living within and for the assurance to Jesus of the joy experienced by those who listened to him. In this sense we can deduce that the gospel brings joy to all who receive it. So, although joy may be experienced in many other of life's experiences, such as the chatter of a baby, or the taste of a good vintage wine, *it is a guaranteed by-product of the gospel of Jesus.* Even suffering can bring joy (Acts 5:41). So, if we're Christians and not experiencing joy, perhaps there's something missing?

The jailer brought them into his house and set a meal before them; he was filled with joy because he had come to believe in God–he and his whole household. (Acts 16:34)

Perhaps we have lost something, perhaps the new wine has become corked? It was well sour at the Church of the Holy Sepulchre, beaten down by religious duty. Even though there may have been the *appearance* of joy as they touched the cracked stone, it came from a false premise of blessings associated with dead stone, rather than the real blessings that we, the *living stones*, can pour into each other. Perhaps we need a reminder. I certainly had one at the Western Wall, with the realisation of how the joy that I witnessed there will be magnified n-fold when 'all Israel shall be saved' and that the dancing and singing will be prompted by the rediscovery of their Messiah, rather than the weekly blessing of the Sabbath.

Joy isn't just associated with the Sabbath for Jewish people. There is a Jewish festival called *Simchat Torah*. It was accidentally experienced one day by none other than the diarist Samuel Pepys on the 14th October 1683, when he stumbled upon a synagogue service in East London. Here are some of his observations in his own words.

… after dinner my wife and I, by Mr. Rawlinson's conduct, to the Jewish Synagogue: where the men and boys in their vayles (tallit), and the women behind a lattice out of sight; and some things stand up, which I believe is their Law (Torah scroll), in a press to which all coming in do bow; and at the putting on their vayles do say something, to which others that hear him do cry Amen, and the party do kiss his vayle. Their service all in a singing way, and in Hebrew. And anon their Laws that they take out of the press are carried by several men, four or five several burthens in all, and they do relieve one another; and whether it is that every one desires to have the carrying of it, I cannot tell, thus they carried it round about the room while such a service is singing. And in the end they had a prayer for the King, which they pronounced his name in Portugall; but the prayer, like the rest, in Hebrew. But, Lord! to see the disorder, laughing, sporting, and no attention, but confusion in all their service, more like brutes than people knowing the true God, would make a man forswear ever seeing them more and indeed I never did see so much, or could have imagined there had been any religion in the whole world so absurdly performed as this. Away thence with my mind strongly disturbed with them, by coach …

Disorder, laughing, confusion! Oh! That our churches could manifest so! Even if we may seem like brutes rather than good polite English gentlemen sitting patiently in the pews! Simchat Torah, *Joy in the Law*. It's the festival to revere the Word of God and, according to the Chabad Jewish website, is characterised by "utterly unbridled joy". The Torah has a high place in the Jewish religious hierarchy and is the source of great joy. And so it should be, as the Psalms tell us so:

The precepts of the LORD are right, giving joy to the heart. The commands of the LORD are radiant, giving light to the eyes. (Psalm 19:8)

Your statutes are my heritage forever; they are the joy of my heart. (Psalm 119:111)

To the left of the Western Wall is a tunnel that runs along a continuation of the wall. This tunnel is a *yeshiva* of sorts, also a synagogue of sorts. It is beyond characterisation as it is basically where serious Torah Jews hang out to study and worship. While I was there, various Shabbat services were being performed, with Torah scrolls removed from ornate cabinets, then carried around briefly so that others could kiss them. One of them was a huge metallic affair, reminiscent of a bomb casing. It opened on vertical hinges, revealing the ancient scroll within, which was lifted up and revealed to onlookers to revere. Then it was placed on a table and a call went out for a *Chazan* (singer) to start the service.

Up stepped a tall, slim, dark fellow in flowing robes, a young man with a beautiful voice. The service started (as did others randomly throughout the length of the tunnel) and many took turns to read from the Holy Scripture. Here was true unity, people who (mostly) have never met and would never meet under any other circumstances, because they were just too different. There were the ultra-orthodox with the furry hat, lesser degrees of orthodox Jew, secular Jews, some in shorts, Ethiopians, Russians and native born Israelis. What united them was far superior than what could divide them. United by their love of the Torah and the joy that it gave them. One young man stood separate from the throng. To me he looked like the sort of "lunatic" perhaps attracted by the surroundings. He was slim, with loose fitting clothes, sandals, dreadlocked hair and a woollen hat. He looked more Rasta than Rabba. The congregational leader then called for more readers ... and up he stepped and read his portion reverently in beautiful Hebrew. Appearances are deceptive.

While experiencing these little episodes at the Western Wall, I continually marked off in my mind a comparison with Gentile Church and, again after again, wondered what the Church has lost when it made a conscious decision many centuries ago to jettison its Hebraic roots in favour of exotic pagan aberrations. Can we learn from these Jews? Can we just catch a flavour of the joy in worship, in reading God's Word, in the fellowship and family relationships that are displayed for the world to see in that huge cultural viewing gallery known as the *Kotel* (Western Wall)?

The Hebrew word for *joy* is *"simcha"*, we have already seen it used in *"Simchat Torah", the joy of the Torah*. What you may have picked up is a major difference between the expressions of joy as experienced within Judaism and with Christians. With Jews, the accent is always on *community*, Simchat Torah is not a festival one celebrates in solitary. The Jewish festivals, as listed in Leviticus 23, are days of joy, of collective celebration.

And rejoice before the LORD your God at the place he will choose as a dwelling for his Name—you, your sons and daughters, your male and female servants, the Levites in your towns, and the foreigners, the fatherless and the widows living among you. (Deuteronomy 16:11)

In Western thought (and by extension, Christian

thought), personal happiness is often stated as the great goal in life. In fact Aristotle said as much, happiness is the ultimate goal at which all humans aim. Then, of course, is the American Declaration of Independence, "the inalienable rights are ... life, liberty and the pursuit of happiness".

But it is not a Biblical imperative, as much as joy is, in the sense that the joy experienced within community is preferable to the happiness experienced by the individual. In his article, *"The Pursuit of Joy"*, Lord Jonathan Sachs says this:

"Happiness is an attitude to life as a whole, while joy lives in the moment. As J. D. Salinger once said: "Happiness is a solid, joy is a liquid." Happiness is something you pursue. But joy is not. It discovers you. It has to do with a sense of connection to other people or to God. It comes from a different realm than happiness. It is a social emotion. It is the exhilaration we feel when we merge with others. It is the redemption of solitude."

The communal nature of joy in the Jewish community is reflected in the very name given to social occasions, such as weddings, *barmitzvahs* or engagement parties. The word is ... *simcha* itself!

Psalm 32:11 begins, *"rejoice in the Lord ..."*. The Hebrew is *samach* (simcha) *Yahweh* (God). It is a command for all of God's people, so let us learn together how to tear down our British reserve and enter into it!

Chaim

18

I have just read the first novel, The Legacy, by the well-known cultural commentator, Melanie Phillips. As a secular Jew, the novel reflected the journey she has undoubtedly been on and, although there is no religious angle in the novel, the portraits she paints of Jewish cultural life are evocative. She parallels three stories, in England in the 12th Century, Poland in the 1940s and modern-day London. Despite the geographical and historical disparities the theme of strong, moral, family-centred life connects all three and it is clear that the author feels a sentimental pull of the certainties of Jewish family life in a world that is doing its best to destroy such a *regressive patriarchal out-dated structure!*

If there is one word that comes to mind it is "life", the triumph of the human spirit over adversity, persecution and hatred. Think of the wedding celebration in "Fiddler on the Roof", the Sabbath throng at the Western Wall or Passovers being celebrated by Auschwitz inmates. Of course, Jews don't have a monopoly here, but there is something about adversity that binds a community together and where there is a shared communal experience, there is life. And arguably, Jews have such a far deeper experience of adversity, in fact much of their four thousand years of experience has been as pariahs, that they can honestly say, *done that, got the t-shirt*. It's a slap in the face of their persecutors, even death itself, by declaring that *life is so precious that we will survive whatever the odds and we are going to savour every minute of it.*

When I was growing up I was introduced to a Hebrew word, *chaim*. My father always told me that it's the *joi de vive* that Jewish people have in abundance, particularly when they get together. I never really understood this as I knew many miserable sour-faced Jews, just as I also came across vivacious and sparkling Gentiles, my wife Monica being a good example. This word *chaim* simply means "life" and Jews use it when making a toast with wine. *L'chaim*, they exclaim, *to Life!* This exclamation is never made over water and some rabbis have an interesting explanation for this. They say that the Hebrew letter most associated with Jews is the *yod*. The word for wine is *yayin*, which has two yods, alluding to Jews coming together in celebration. The word for water, *mayim*, only has a single yod, and *"... it is not good for a human being to be alone"!*

Let's consider that declaration from Deuteronomy 30:

This day I call the heavens and the earth as witnesses against you that I have set before you life and death, blessings and curses. Now choose life, so that you and your children may live and that you may love the LORD your God, listen to his voice, and hold fast to him. For the LORD is your life, and he will give you many years in the land he swore to give to your fathers, Abraham, Isaac and Jacob. (Deuteronomy 30:19-20)

How frustrating it is to read this "after the event". Why couldn't Moses' generation have just listened to these words? All they had to do is realise that their lives were in the Lord's Hands and all they had to do was be faithful to Him. Was it such a big thing to listen to Him? How history could have been kinder to them if they had? Well, we can't change history but we certainly can claim this Scripture for ourselves and *choose life,* as the rules ain't changed because He hasn't changed.

Is there *chaim* in our churches? Of course, one can't

speak for every church everywhere, but here's a general observation. Church congregations tend to be artificial communities of people brought together because of a shared experience of Jesus, but mostly without shared backgrounds, culture and so on. One often gets the impression that there is more to divide them than to unite them. It is as if there's a missing ingredient, one that would bring them together in stronger ways. Jews have two candidates for this, a shared background and culture and also a shared experience of persecution. It is a community that has a justified paranoia complex, *they really are out to get us!*

Chaim seems to be stronger in church congregations that are under strong direct persecution, as we occasionally see on videos smuggled out of such places as Iran and China. For them, their faith is a life or death decision and freely celebrate the former because they know that the latter can come at any time. Ironically persecution can become a blessing. If it ever came to Western churches (and there's every indication that this is a very strong possibility the way our society is progressing) we will be forced to take our faith very seriously indeed. Gone will be church-as-social-club as those people would melt under the first whiff of trouble and, indeed, whole churches will compromise themselves out of meaningful existence and will acquiesce to whatever the State is telling them to do. Then, with what's left we shall see true *chaim*. Perhaps we will finally have a Church that resembles the Church of the early Roman Empire, when persecution was extreme. The Christian and the Jewish experience will at last have something in common, a true community experience born out of adversity, where life suddenly becomes very precious and is therefore celebrated.

How will this look? Two areas initially come to mind, music and dance. A recent experience of mine showcases both of these. It was the 2018 *Klezmer* in the Park festival in Regent's Park, London. *Klezmer* is a Jewish musical genre that was born in the shtetls of Eastern Europe a few centuries ago. It is the very embodiment of *chaim*, a quote about it declares, *klezmer* captures all who hear it weep, sing, sigh and celebrate. It beautifully expresses the joys and pains of life. You only have to consider the principal instruments within its arsenal, the clarinet, the violin, the accordion and – of course – the human voice. In fact, the musicians often coax their instruments into replicas of the latter, with sobs, wails and whoops of delight. The word *klezmer* only appeared in the 1930s and is a Hebrew word for "vessel of song".

The festival was a celebration of *klezmer* and featured musicians and groups from all over Europe, not all of them Jewish. The music is not just for listening to, but is intended to get people onto their feet in dance. Most people were on their feet, with some swaying and tapping of feet, but the real spectacle was the lines of dancers weaving through the crowd in formation. All ages, all levels of skill, a celebration of chaim, even when the songs were sad and mournful.

Klezmer is very much an audible extension of the Jewish experience, bittersweet and raw, compelling and triumphant. By way of contrast, what has the Gentile Church given us? Undoubtedly beautiful music. From Gregorian Chants, the various Mass expressions, Hymns to Carols, we have music for the mind and spirit, particularly when there is singing in the vernacular. With contemporary Praise and Worship music we have nothing unique, just a Christian expression of popular secular rock and folk music. Yet, with the exception of the Negro (am

I allowed to say this word?) Spirituals, also born out of personal adversity, *klezmer* is unique, as a musical genre founded on tears, but transcending its origins. Of course we must hold back on the eulogies and snap back into reality but it is worth sparing some thoughts on the role of music in our worship to God.

As I have written about extensively (most of my last few books), *worship*, despite common usage, is not all about music. A worship *genre* has appeared that gives this impression, fuelled by the forms of worship leaders, worship service, worship CDs, that can skew the *function* of giving worship to the Lord, through all of the gifts He has given us. If music focusses our attention on the Lord, *and Him only,* then it is performing its prescribed function. But if it is used to highlight the skills (and behaviour) of worship leaders on a platform, or to emotionally manipulate an audience, or as a 'warm up' before the preacher hits the platform, then it is just another way that *the world and its ways have crept into the Church.*

On the other hand if music, whatever it is, can facilitate our walk with God, then go for it! And if it can do so in the spirit of *chaim*, all the better. I'm still waiting to hear *klezmer* music in a church, they really don't know what they are missing! Can you imagine a *klezmer* treatment of the Psalms, for instance?

Then there is dance. If the music promotes *chaim*, then, if limbs are in reasonable working order, dance is sure to follow. And nothing fits the bill better than Hebraic dance. Here's what I wrote in **Livin' the Life**:

Davidic or Hebraic Dance. There is something very special here, as evidenced by the number of people set free and blessed at our conferences through Hebraic dance.

To understand more about such dance let us first compare it with other forms of dance. Folk dancing is a social activity performed for personal enjoyment. Israeli dancing is a form of folk dancing with Hebraic elements, but again performed for personal enjoyment. But Davidic or Hebraic dancing is different. It is performed as an act of worship, for individual dancers but also for the observers. It is danced primarily for the glory of God.

There are set steps and positions in Hebraic dance. Each is significant and shows a different aspect of worship to God. All steps have meaning and so are performed in a gesture of worship to God. This is not personal expression, a feature of most forms of modern dance, but rather a calculated expression of devotion to the Divine. Yoga is basically the same thing, but devotion, even when not intended or realised, is to something very far from divine.

We have had many testimonies of folk, particularly men, who have been set free by Hebraic dance at our Foundations conferences. People have danced for the first time in Church, having previously being told of its unseemly nature among God's people. In one of our Foundation days, I, along with over twenty others, danced in clumsy gay abandon and felt quite good about it too. Our wonderful dance teachers, Ginnie and Rosie of the *Sh'ma Kingdom dancers*, don't just encourage non-dancers to dance and experienced dancers to dance even better, but they create great tableaux of dance, with dramas that tear at the Spirit and point us to the *chaim* that really should be part of the normal church experience. For an example, have a look at the dramatic performance of *Glory Battle* at High Leigh at https://www.youtube.com/watch?v=DrWl-fdRSc4&t=10s

Our current culture in the West encourages individual aspiration rather than collective responsibility. We have been taught to look inwards and strive for personal happiness above all, rather than looking outwards and perhaps missing out on the *simcha* experienced in true community living. In a recent theatre experience refugees from the Calais "Jungle" camp were brought over to resettle in the UK. After some time, one of them was so unhappy with what he saw as the soulless Western life and pined for the community he experienced in the camp, despite the deprivations there. In Hebrew thought, community - *kehillah* – is all important, this is where, as we have seen, *chaim* is expressed. It is so important that, in Judaism, the Jews are primarily self-defined not as a religion, but as a people, *Am Yisrael*, the people of Israel. Perhaps if the Church did the same, unity could be encouraged, perhaps even attained (once doctrinal differences have been hammered out)! But, then again, no other people in history have been forged as a nation as a result of a few repeated words at the foot of a mountain. Of course this was an extra special one-off, with a couple of million of the Hebrew people receiving the Torah at the foot of Mount Sinai from God Himself. *"... and God spoke all of these words"* (Exodus 20:1).

When Abraham moved location, he took his whole extended family with him. As did Joseph, helping to resettle his wider family in Egypt. The Hebrews, now formed as a nation, moved together as a people, the wider community was far more important than personal ambition. To be excluded from community was one of the greatest punishments that could be inflicted for crimes committed. Leviticus 20 has a whole list of such crimes, such as chasing after foreign gods. They would be "cut off from their people". This phrase appears over twenty times in the Torah and it highlights the high esteem that was held for living in community.

Since Bible times, Jews have continued living in community, ironically aided by the persecution from the Christians. In the Talmud there is an instruction about the minimum requirements for such a community.

"A scholar is not allowed to live in a city that does not have these 10 things: a beit din (law court) that metes out punishments; a tzedakah fund that is collected by two people and distributed by three; a synagogue; a bath house (mikveh); a bathroom; a doctor; a craftsperson; a blood-letter; (some versions add: a butcher); and a teacher of children." (Sanhedrin 17b)

Mind, body and spirit are all catered for in the above list. One suspects that a modern list would run into the hundreds and include such items as flat screen TV, fridge freezers and games consoles, to highlight our current need for our comforts. When Jews arrived in London at the end of the 19th Century, fleeing the pogroms of Eastern Europe, they followed the principle of landsleit, creating small communities, perhaps within the space of a few houses, as a mirror image of what they have left behind, the minimum requirement being a synagogue, a ritual bath and a source of kosher food. Around two hundred synagogues appeared around this time in the Whitechapel square mile. This shows the importance of religious living. Community was all well and good, but it also had to be well with God.

Are our churches true communities? What makes them different from social clubs, labour clubs or friendship societies? Unfortunately, many are no different from their secular counterparts. The key factor is that the central purpose must be paramount. *All must be well with God.* When persecution comes we are going to need a community, a **kehillah**, bound together by a single purpose, whatever its ethnic or social mix, to be God's ambassadors to a society that has reasoned Him out of existence.

Kadosh   19

I am the LORD, who brought you up out of Egypt to be your God; therefore be holy, because I am holy. (Leviticus 11:45)

Of course we are called to be holy, this is a persistent theme throughout the Bible and we have had much teaching on this subject, though most of us would be honest enough to admit that practice has rarely matched theory. What I want us to think about instead is the Holiness of God Himself. The Hebrew word is *Kadosh*. The Paul Wilbur song of the same name simply states Who He is, *the Lord of hosts, Who was and Who is and Who is to come*.

I believe that many in the Church today have lost sight of this. Here are a few pointers, as listed in Hebraic Church:

- Celebrations/events are planned and advertised with catchy slogans promising what God is going to do there, *so you must not miss the blessing*. We simply can't treat our Creator as if He's just another celebrity coming to do His act. Of course, He is gracious enough to turn up at these places despite our efforts, simply because He always wishes to bless individuals. It's just a shame that these ministries take the credit for this!

- TV evangelists / faith preachers. Do I really need to say more?

- When unusual natural disasters occur the default response of the mainstream Church is to assure the world that this has nothing to do with God. Have they not read their Bibles and seen how God has often used the elements as warning signs to His people? Or do they believe that God has turned into a polite civilised Englishman?

• The ready acceptance of our churchmen to follow a "scientific" narrative when explaining the world rather than the unchangeable Word of God.

• The shameful treatment of the Jewish people, something that still runs as a niggling undercurrent through the UK Church. To deny a continuing relationship of Jews with their God is to deny God's covenants with mankind, which is tantamount to calling Him fickle, or a liar.

• The current accent on 'God is Love', categorising Him as purely one-dimensional and denying a full understanding of our multifaceted Creator. The widespread lack of Old Testament knowledge is responsible for this inexcusable ignorance. Isn't it better to acknowledge Him as a person and not a philosophical abstract and instead describe Him as God *Who* loves.

What about the Jewish experience? To answer this, we open our Bibles in the Hebrew Scriptures, in the Book of Exodus, chapter twenty, the *Ten Commandments* or, to be more precise, the "Ten Sayings". This makes sense when we look at the first "saying", as Christianity and Judaism are at odds as *to what this actually is!*

The Rabbis declare the first "saying" as the contents of Exodus 20:2:

I am the LORD your God, who brought you out of Egypt, out of the land of slavery.

This is a saying, a declaration, it is *not* a commandment. This is why the Christians disregard this and simply take this as a prelude to what they say is the first "commandment", Exodus 20:3.

Why is this relevant? It is because, to the Jews, it is *a declaration of Who God is*. Everything else flows from this.

The sheer fact of this dwarfs all that follows. You can imagine the scene, at the foot of Sinai. The Hebrews are actually hearing God's voice, and these are the first words they hear:
I am the LORD your God, who brought you out of Egypt, out of the land of slavery.
Can you imagine their reaction? Awe doesn't do it justice, or any word that we can dig out of our reserve of superlatives. Perhaps a mighty booming voice, or perhaps a still small voice? Whatever, the Source of these words would be unmistakeable.

Just consider the first part, expressed in the Hebrew words, *Anoki Adonai Elohekha*. The first word takes the meaning "I am", but this very word is mainly used in the context of a *royal* command. Its literal meaning is *Because I Am* and is used over a hundred times in Scripture. Remember, It is God Himself speaking here and we're not to forget that. It underlines all that follows and puts a Divine seal on the sayings that follow. These aren't *ordinary* instructions, these are part of God's Word of life for us!

Remember God's answer to Moses from the burning bush (Exodus 3:14), when He was asked to identify Himself. *I am that I AM (or I will BE)*.

God just ... is. He is the Creator, the Source, the Sustainer, the Redeemer. He doesn't need a whole bunch of words to describe Himself. He is God, everything and everyone else just revolves around that awesome fact.

The point about all of this is that I believe that the Rabbis have an understanding of this *Kadosh* that the Church has failed to grasp. Let's move to the next "saying", the Second Saying for the Jews, the First Commandment for the Christians.

"You shall have no other gods before me. (Exodus 12:3)
Other gods were certainly an issue in the formative

years, in fact the vast number of instructions in the Torah were there to help the Hebrews follow this one, by offering harsh punishments as deterrents. Of course now, *other gods* have been packaged as rival religions, such as Hinduism and Buddhism and are no longer a direct threat to orthodox Judaism, though they are a great issue for Christianity, as roadblocks against the Great Commission.

Nevertheless, it is heartbreakingly sad, when considering the shared history of the Jewish people and their "Christian" oppressors that the idea of "Jesus" had been so corrupted by his so-called followers that he was considered by the Jews as *another god* and many measures had been taken by the rabbis to protect their people from this "imposter". To this end, a prayer was composed in the Second Century:

"May the slanderers have no hope; and may all wickedness perish in an instant; and may all of our enemies be cut down speedily. May you speedily uproot, smash, cast down and humble the arrogant sinners – speedily in our days. Blessed are You, O Lord, who breaks enemies and humbles arrogant sinners."

Jewish Christians were even known as *minim*, heretics, by their estranged brethren. Other names given to them by Jewish religious leaders include *apikoresim* (heretics) or *meshummadin* (apostates) but it was the names given to Jesus himself that really raised the ante. The Talmud referred to him as *Yeshu*, that may seem an affectionate shortening of his Hebrew name, *Yeshua*, but, in fact, was an acronym for the Hebrew expression *yemach shemo vezichro*, which means, *"may his name and memory be obliterated"*.

Of course none of this would have happened if the Christians had only implemented Paul's wishes for *One New Man*, with Jew and Gentile in peace and in brotherhood!

It was the next commandment/saying which really addresses the issue of *Kadosh* and highlights which of God's people were really taking His holiness seriously.

You shall not make for yourself an image in the form of anything in heaven above or on the earth beneath or in the waters below. You shall not bow down to them or worship them; for I, the LORD your God, am a jealous God ... (Exodus 20:4-5)

To see how this one has worked out one should compare two buildings, both built at the same time and barely a couple of miles apart; Christopher Wren's St Paul's Cathedral, consecrated for use in 1697 and Bevis Marks synagogue, built in 1701, the oldest surviving synagogue in the UK.

A tour of St Paul's brings us face to face with many images, from the gargoyles and cherubim around the outside; to the depiction of the conversion of Paul, with other apostles and evangelists looking on; to the ornate and adorned high altar; to the memorials and coffins of Nelson, Wellington, Wren and others; to the sculptures of St Michael and St George and the Virgin Mary and an effigy of Lord Kitchener; to the military banners and flags; to the religious art and stained glass windows.

Bevis Marks synagogue has none, just lots of candles, gleaming metal and wooden benches, the only ostentations being the renaissance-style ark containing the Torah scrolls and the seven hanging brass candelabra.

No prizes to guessing which of the two was most mindful of Exodus 20:4. There is actually a word that encapsulates the principle behind this command, *aniconism*, literally "no-image-ism" in Greek. The rabbis are very mindful of the *golden calf* incident and prophets such as Isaiah, Jeremiah and Amos would warn again and again about idolatry. The *Kadosh* of God was paramount and there were too many instances when Divine punishment followed any dalliances with "other gods". Although the warning is given in Exodus 20:4, it is the following verse that proclaims the consequences of bowing down and worshipping the images. It is never wise to disrespect our jealous God. Of course, if the images are not there in the first place …!

The acknowledgement of the commandment not to create images stretched right through to post-Bible Jewish history, in the design of synagogues right up to modern times.

In the Church, aniconism has been held onto a little lighter, with not such a firm adherence to the commandment. There were two periods in history when a reaction sprung forth against the depiction of images and icons within churches. These reactions were called *iconoclasms*, "icon destruction", and the first was in Byzantine Europe in the Eighth and Ninth Century, as a result of theological argument based on Greek philosophical ideas rather than the Laws of Moses. The second was the Protestant Reformation, when many churches were ransacked and pictures, statues and other objects of "adoration" pulled down and desecrated, as a reaction against Catholic excesses and dubious practices. As St Paul's Cathedral, a centre of Anglicanism in London, is a by-product of the Reformation, one can see a relaxation of this attitude, with social convention trumping any realisation of the Kadosh of God and any adherence to one of the Ten Commandments.

The next commandment/saying is Exodus 20:7:

You shall not misuse the name of the LORD your God, for the LORD will not hold anyone guiltless who misuses his name.

It's the one about blasphemy. Breaking this one had consequences:

Say to the Israelites: 'If anyone curses his God, he will be held responsible; anyone who blasphemes the name of the LORD must be put to death. The entire assembly must stone him. Whether an alien or native-born, when he blasphemes the Name, he must be put to death'. (Leviticus 24:15-16)

It's as well we are not under the Old Covenant in terms of *consequences* of actions, otherwise the world would be a very lonely place, inhabited only by a few maiden aunts and the odd vicar, because the rest of us would have been stoned to death for blasphemy!

But I've never taken the name of God in vain in any way! Yes you have. Here are some euphemisms for "God"; *by gad, oh my gosh, by gum, by Jove, by George, so 'elp me Bob, by Godfrey, great Scott, good grief, goodness gracious, begorrah,* We've all uttered one or two of these in our time, haven't we?

Have we taken the Lord's name in vain? Of course we have, though, in mitigation, we mostly haven't realised it, or have felt safe in the knowledge that a *derivation is not the actual word, so no worries!* I wonder what God thinks? Yet even Christians have been known to utter such epithets as "Oh my God!" or "Oh God". These may not be seen as blasphemies, but perhaps can be suggested as over-familiarity with the Deity. The use of the phrase "Jesus Christ!" in all of its derivations seems to be on the rise in popular dramas, even our daytime soaps. We don't need euphemisms these days as there is no guilty conscience or penalties in uttering blasphemies. That's a good indication that our society today is very much *Post-Christian.*

And what of the Jewish experience? The rabbis have always taken the punishments described in Leviticus 24 seriously with regards to taking the Lord's name in vain. Whereas "Christian" society in the UK has produced a whole catalogue of euphemisms that are thinly-veiled substitutes for the Lord's name, Jews go a lot further. It goes back to the Masoretes, the Jewish scholars who compiled the definitive Hebrew Old Testament in the 10th Century AD and it concerns the sacred name of God, *YHWH*, when it appears in Scripture.

It was the Name never to be pronounced, because of the Commandment. But the Masoretes' job was to add vowels to all words and make them *pronounceable*. What they did was to use the vowels from the word ***Adonai*** (Lord) and splice them into YHWH. The reason for this is that Jewish readers would be reminded to use the word *Adonai*, rather than YHWH, *thus not breaking the commandment*. The early English translators of the Bible were unaware of what the Masoretes had done and also had no fear themselves about uttering the sacred Name, so they translated *exactly* what they saw. They ended up with *Jehovah*. And thus a new name for God was produced, an *incorrect one*. The rest, as they say, is history.

What of today? What is the acceptable attitude today among Christians? Are we bound by the sensibilities of those Jews who declared that the Name of God was unutterable or do we attempt to say His name, but at least *get it right?* Orthodox Jews today NEVER ever write the name "God" or even "Lord" and replace the vowel with a hyphen, writing it thus, "G-d" or "L-rd". In speech they use other terms. A popular one is ***Ha Shem*** (The Name). There is even one used by Matthew, the Gospel writer specifically writing to the Jewish people of his day. When speaking of the Kingdom that Jesus had come to initiate, all other writers used the expression "Kingdom of God". In Matthew's case, although he used this expression four times, he used another one 34 times, the only Gospel writer to do so. He used the expression, *Kingdom of Heaven*. This avoided using the word "God" and used instead the euphemism, *Heaven*.

So, the first four "sayings" in Exodus 20 remind us of the *Kadosh*, holiness, of God. To remind you:

And God spoke all these words: "I am the LORD your God, who brought you out of Egypt, out of the land of slavery. You shall have no other gods before me. You shall not make for yourself an image in the form of anything in heaven above or on the earth beneath or in the waters below ... You shall not misuse the name of the LORD your God, for the LORD will not hold anyone guiltless who misuses his name."

There is one more saying, in the next few verses, that is concerned with our responsibilities towards God Himself:

"Remember the Sabbath day by keeping it holy ..." (Exodus 20:8)

So Sabbath is also a matter of *Kadosh*. We have already discussed this but now perhaps we can start to think again and wonder why it is the only one of the ten commandments/sayings that is deliberately not followed by some Christians. *This one is really between you and your God.*

Chesed   20

This is a truly wonderful word. It is a Biblical word that appears over two hundred and forty times in the Hebrew Scriptures, twenty six times in Psalm 136 alone! What makes it special is that, over all the main Bible translations, there are documented over a hundred and sixty different possible meanings of *chesed*.

The King James version (as well as the Jewish Publication Society) plumps mainly for *mercy*. The New International Version veers towards *love*, the NAS prefers *lovingkindness*, the ESV has *steadfast love*, as does the NRV. Each of these translations, as well as all others, also have a whole list of secondary meanings too.

Apparently, it's all down to context, the circumstances that surround its use. Yet, the question persists, what is its core meaning? After all, as with most Hebrew words, it is based on a three letter root word, from which one ought to gather its primary meaning (for more on this subject you could read **God's Signature**). There are two aspects to *chesed*, a big meaning and a little meaning. The big meaning is when the word is used in the context of God's dealings with man and the little meaning is used for man's dealings with man. First the big meaning …

Before we do this, I think the major point here that the theologians seem to be missing, is that we have no right to dissect our God and explore His character and motivations, neither do we have the mental facilities to do so. We can try our best, which is the inclination of the Greek Mindset, but the Hebrew Mindset would just shrug its shoulders and say, *God is God, leave Him alone and just bask in His Greatness.* Perhaps the reason why *chesed* is so flexible and confusing to interpret, is that it was never meant to be interpreted. *It is just an expression of His Godness.*

Yet, if there's one word that could possibly be the best fit, it is *magnanimity,* going above and beyond what is expected. Let's think more about this ...

God does not live in a box, or a church or temple, He cannot be confined by us in space, neither can He be confined by us in character. There's a perfectly good reason why not all are healed, not all are saved, good people don't always flourish all the time or bad people get away with bad things some of the time. The reason is *God,* the God who does things His way, for His purposes, in His time. This is the God of the unexpected and also the God who, by our standards, is forever going above and beyond the expected, through His *chesed.*

First here are six familiar examples of His chesed in the Psalms:

But I trust in your unfailing love (chesed); my heart rejoices in your salvation. (Psalm 13:5)

The LORD loves righteousness and justice; the earth is full of his unfailing love (chesed) (Psalm 33:5)

Do not withhold your mercy from me, LORD; may your love (chesed) and faithfulness always protect me. (Psalm 40:11)

Because your love (chesed) is better than life, my lips will glorify you. (Psalm 63:3)

I will declare that your love (chesed) stands firm forever, that you have established your faithfulness in heaven itself. (Psalm 89:2)

Give thanks to the LORD, for he is good. His love (chesed) endures forever. (Psalm 136:1)

The NIV uses the word *love* in these instances because the English language doesn't have a stronger, deeper word that could do justice, so love is the best fit, just as the KJV uses the word *mercy*, the NAS uses *lovingkindness* and so on. Perhaps we should simply use the word *chesed*, as a new word in the lexicon, as that unknowable characteristic of God whereby He does the most wonderful things that we simply can't get our heads around?

We don't have to think hard to look for practical examples of God's *chesed* to us, times when He has gone *above and beyond the expected.*

He showed His chesed when:

• He promised Abraham an unconditional covenant despite the unworthiness of his descendants

The LORD appeared to Isaac and said, "Do not go down to Egypt; live in the land where I tell you to live. Stay in this land for a while, and I will be with you and will bless you. For to you and your descendants I will give all these lands and will confirm the oath I swore to your father Abraham. I will make your descendants as numerous as the stars in the sky and will give them all these lands, and through your offspring all nations on earth will be blessed, because Abraham obeyed me and did everything I required of him, keeping my commands, my decrees and my instructions." (Genesis 26:2-5)

• He didn't wipe out the Hebrews despite their idolatry

"I have seen these people," the LORD said to Moses, "and they are a stiff-necked people. Now leave me alone so that my anger may burn against them and that I may destroy them. Then I will make you into a great nation." But Moses sought the favour of the LORD his God. "LORD," he said, "why should your anger burn against your people, whom you brought out of Egypt with great power and a mighty hand? Why should the Egyptians say, 'It was with evil intent that he brought them out, to kill them in the mountains and to wipe them off the face of the earth'? Turn from your fierce anger; relent and do not bring disaster on your

people. *Remember your servants Abraham, Isaac and Israel, of whom you swore by your own self: 'I will make your descendants as numerous as the stars in the sky and I will give your descendants all this land I promised them, and it will be their inheritance forever.'" Then the LORD relented and did not bring on his people the disaster he had threatened.* (Exodus 32:9-14)

- He ensured that a remnant within Judah would survive despite their sins

Nevertheless, for the sake of his servant David, the LORD was not willing to destroy Judah. He had promised to maintain a lamp for David and his descendants forever. (2 Kings 8:19)

- He died for us on the cross

But God demonstrates his own love for us in this: While we were still sinners, Christ died for us. (Romans 5:8)

All of these were way beyond anything we would do, which is why they are aspects of a Divine quality, *chesed*, that we could never grasp with our human minds.

Then there's the other aspect of *chesed*, the little meaning, addressing the relationship between man and man. This is the popular usage of chesed within the Jewish community, fuelled by the Jewish Publication Society (JPS) translation of the word as *mercy*.

This manifests as acts of kindness and charity, something that is very much a feature of Jewish society. These are not the acts of charity, such as giving to the poor, that are considered a duty. These are known as *tzedakah*, a religious obligation. Rather, *chesed* represents acts of kindness and charity that go above and beyond the expected and can be directed to anyone, even the rich and the undeserving. Subsequently many Jewish charitable initiatives make use of the word 'chesed' in their titles. How about Biblical examples? A good place to start is the Sermon on the Mount:

"*You have heard that it was said, 'Eye for eye, and tooth for tooth.' But I tell you, do not resist an evil person. If anyone slaps you on the right cheek, turn to them the other cheek also. And if anyone wants to sue you and take your shirt, hand over your coat as well. If anyone forces you to go one mile, go with them two miles. Give to the one who asks you, and do not turn away from the one who wants to borrow from you. "You have heard that it was said, 'Love your neighbour and hate your enemy.' But I tell you, love your enemies and pray for those who persecute you, that you may be children of your Father in heaven. He causes his sun to rise on the evil and the good, and sends rain on the righteous and the unrighteous. If you love those who love you, what reward will you get? Are not even the tax collectors doing that? And if you greet only your own people, what are you doing more than others? Do not even pagans do that? Be perfect, therefore, as your heavenly Father is perfect.* (Matthew 5:38-48)

This is *chesed* galore. This is also a picture of God's *chesed*, by demonstrating to us how difficult is is to *go beyond*. Turning the other cheek, handing over your coat, going the extra mile, giving freely, loving your enemy, praying for your persecutor! This is a glimpse into God's world, being empowered by the Holy Spirit to do wonderful things, as a demonstration of the new life we have in Christ. And it's chesed that drives it all!

For Old Testament examples we just need to look at two short books, Ruth and Hosea. In Ruth we have this Moabitess showing extraordinary love and favour towards her Jewish mother-in-law, Naomi.

But Ruth replied, "Don't urge me to leave you or to turn back from you. Where you go I will go, and where you stay I will stay. Your people will be my people and your God my God. Where you die I will die, and there I will be buried. May the LORD deal with me, be it ever so severely, if even death separates you and me." (Ruth 1:16-17)

This is certainly going above and beyond. Ruth is

showing *chesed* towards Naomi, a selfless and altruistic act.

Hosea was asked by God to show extraordinary *chesed* towards his wife, despite her persistent unfaithfulness.

The LORD said to me, "Go, show your love to your wife again, though she is loved by another man and is an adulteress. Love her as the LORD loves the Israelites, though they turn to other gods and love the sacred raisin cakes." So I bought her for fifteen shekels of silver and about a homer and a lethek of barley. Then I told her, "You are to live with me many days; you must not be a prostitute or be intimate with any man, and I will behave the same way toward you." (Hosea 3:1-3)

Of course, this is a picture of God's greater *chesed* towards His unfaithful people, but Hosea still had to go through it!

So there it is. *Chesed* is probably not a word you've ever heard of and many theologians and translators were so flummoxed by it that they have put forward an extensive collection of possible meanings, to cover all bases. It is really quite simple as *chesed* is probably the defining characteristic of God. It is His *chesed* and, when we become one with Him, we also inherit *chesed*, enabling us to go above and beyond, as we saw in the Sermon on the Mount.

The problem has been, as ever, the Greek mindset that we, and particularly our academics, have inherited. The Greek mind strives for understanding and when it hits something that, perhaps, is not meant for our understanding, then it flounders and panics. *Chesed* is the case in point and, by confusing the issue for the rest of us with a whole dictionary of possible meanings, they have ensured that we remain in ignorance about it. Doesn't it seem odd that a word that is so prevalent and important in the Hebrew Scriptures is not one that we are familiar with? Blame the theologians, their Greek minds can't accept that *chesed* is just ... *chesed*. The Hebrew mind accepts this and is quite happy to accept that God has a quality that somehow represents how He is able to remain interested in our flawed humanity and will always go that extra mile for us.

Before we end, here is a friend's testimony, of how an appreciation of God's *chesed* helped him in a very real sense through a major illness:

"Without discovering the true nature of the character of Heavenly Father, I'm not sure how I could have got through the last few decades. I have been struggling as a pituitary tumour has thrown my hormones wildly out of balance, and that led to other things being out of balance in my life. One key to healing came to me while studying 'balance' in the scriptures, and I discovered this wonderful Hebrew word 'chesed'. Many times it occurs when describing Father's character alongside things like His truth, or His justice. For me at the beginning, the key revelation was the translation of it as lovingkindness, or simply kindness.

Put simply, He has been kind to me. I don't mean the tumour has left my body, (although it's affect has begun to be controlled) but He has walked through it with me, and when it has threatened to overwhelm me, I wasn't washed away or drowned, because He reminded me of His strong and kind presence with me as I meditated on the Word. (Isaiah 43:2 "When thou passest through the waters, I will be with thee; and through the rivers, they shall not overflow thee: ...").

You see in the case of the scripture above, it doesn't even include the word chesed, but it does reflect the truth of the revelation of it being Father's true nature. The word chesed occurs often in the Hebrew Scriptures, but it also suffuses the whole of the Holy Bible as Father's true nature is revealed. So there is a huge wealth of scriptures on which to meditate. Of course 'kindness' is not enough to encompass all the riches of God's character, and chesed is translated wonderfully variously, and each word is worth meditating on for a healthy balanced 'diet', but somehow even to this day, kindness is a quality which melts my heart. It seems to be in short supply today, as lives get busier, and people get more preoccupied with meeting the needs of their own small circle. So giving it and receiving it is becoming more and more precious, and a rare and valued expression of the Father's love. But coming to The Lord, His kindness never changes. To help our feeble human minds, in the scriptures it is balanced by His truth, justice and holiness, but that is only necessary because we cannot comprehend true kindness without corrupting it into a weak and pale compromise. But in Heavenly Father, true, strong, pure kindness can be found, and it is a pearl of great price."

One feels that One New Man ought to have no problem with *chesed* and that an understanding of the Hebrew Mindset would have ensured that this word would have been as familiar to us as love. God is *love*. Yes, but God also is *chesed!*

Mishpocha   21

There's an interesting definition of *mishpocha* in the urban dictionary on the web; *an entire family that is very lucky because of their home*. It is right to zero in on the home environment, but luck? Luck doesn't come into it, it is very much a God-thing, but, for the Jews, it was bought at a price. The next few paragraphs are adapted from a more extensive treatment in **How the Church Lost the Way**.

Jewish life through the ages has been bittersweet. The bitterness has been from without, the sweetness from within. Their communities have always lived in a precarious state, never accepted by the Christian world that surrounded them. Yet once the outside world had been shut out, life for ordinary Jews within their own communities had been a million times more meaningful, wholesome and joyful than that of their Christian neighbours. How ironic was that?

While the medieval Christian was living in poverty, ignorance and subservience, kept in place by the promises of the "next world", what of his Jewish neighbour? Let us consider the home. The Jewish home was always intended as a holy place. The Tabernacle in the desert and the Temple in Jerusalem in Biblical times were holy places. They were known as a *miqdash*, meaning "sanctuary", a place set apart for worship of God. When the Temple was destroyed by the Romans, the rabbis declared that every Jewish home should become a holy place, referring to them as a *miqdash me'at*, a "small sanctuary". The home was to be a place for worshipping God, a holy place. Tradition tells us that, when the Temple was destroyed, the *shekinah*, God's Glory, didn't settle in the synagogues, where you would have expected it to, but made its home in every Jewish home. God was truly identifying with the people where they lived. Isn't this a profound yet wonderful thought? While the Christians at that time trapped God in cold, busy, glitzy cathedrals and churches, as the exclusive property of the clergy, with visiting rights granted to the *hoi polloi* every Sunday, in Jewish tradition God was present in the place where they slept, ate and gathered together as families.

Whereas in Christian tradition, the focus for activities is the church building, for the Jew it is the family home. Our home is to be a "house of prayer" for the worship of God. It is to be a "house of study", for the learning of God's Word. It is also to be a "house of assembly", a place where people are welcomed. Added to that it is also to be a "house of eating and drinking", a "house of sleeping", a "house of making love" and so on. Try doing that lot in church, see how far that gets you!

Most Christians travel to church every Sunday and watch as the priest / minister / pastor / vicar conducts various spiritual rituals on their behalf, from administering Holy Communion to the hymn/prayer sandwich, to the thirty minute sermon. Religious Jews, by contrast, are told to "know God in all your ways", which involves every aspect of their lives. Think about religious occasions. Where do Christians celebrate Christmas and Easter? They go to church, at least for the "religious" aspects, the rituals and the liturgy. Where do Jews typically celebrate their religious occasions? In their home. For example, for Jews since Biblical times, Passover is a tightly structured occasion that is firmly anchored in the home environment, from the hunt for *chametz* (leavened bread), which requires a complete cleaning of the home prior to the festival, to the welcoming of strangers to partake of the meal with the family. In the Feast of Tabernacles, *Sukkot*, temporary shelters are built adjoining the home, where at least one meal is eaten and some (in hotter climes than ours) even attempt to sleep in them.

Even the everyday act of eating is celebrated with spiritual connotations. The dinner table corresponds to the altar of the Temple. Does that mean we worship food, an accusation often directed at Jewish people? No, because even eating is a sacred act and the dinner table will also function as a place where words of Godly wisdom are exchanged in the conversations that accompany the eating, where Hebrew prayers resound and songs are sung in praise of their God.

And it's the dinner table that is the central focus. It is where the family assemble for shared meals. It is also where the father imparts his wisdom to the next generation (presumably between mouthfuls):

These commandments that I give you today are to be on your hearts. Impress them on your children. Talk about them when you sit at home and when you walk along the road, when you lie down and when you get up. Tie them as symbols on your hands and bind them on your foreheads. Write them on the doorframes of your houses and on your gates. (Deuteronomy 6:6-9)

It is where families eat together, pray together, study together, chat together, even confess to each other. The father may have the main responsibility of teaching but the mother's role is not to be undervalued, she is the glue that holds it together, sadly a 'divisive' statement to make in the current era of gender confusion. The mother is the home builder, the nurturer, the architect of the systems required for the efficient running of the household (something I witness first-hand with more admiration than I often admit to!). It is the mother who will light the candles and recite the blessing at Sabbath time and also the other festivals. It used to be traditional for the father to recite the following at the start of Sabbath:

A wife of noble character who can find? She is worth far more than rubies. Her husband has full confidence in her and lacks nothing of value. She brings him good, not harm, all the days of her life. (Proverbs 31:10-12)

The dining table is the focus of the festivals and the Sabbath, which is kicked off by the Friday night Shabbat meal. The Passover Seder night has already been mentioned and those who have experienced this, whether as a childhood memory, or as an adapted church celebration, can attest of the 'dining table experience'. This got me thinking and I produced a small book, entitled the **Easter Telling,** instructing Christians how to run their own Passover Seder service, with 'added Jesus', making it an effective and entertaining tool to explain the death and resurrection of Jesus to a small multi-generational group. But it needn't stop there.

I am in the process of doing the same for Christmas (Birth of Christ), Pentecost (*Shavuot*) and Harvest time (*Succoth*/Tabernacles), in essence creating a 'Seder' meal experience for each of them. This is very much in the spirit of One New Man, as it brings Gentile Christians into a Jewish model that could benefit all.

A home is where you can be real, where you are *you*. If we considered our homes in the same way as religious Jews then there would be no room for hypocrisy. We could hardly be "Sunday Christians", wearing our "Sunday best" and reserving our pious religious face for those Sunday moments, then undoing our belt and resuming our bickering with our spouse in the car on the way home! Instead our home becomes our church and God has His beady big eye on us 24/7. Can we handle that? In a way that's irrelevant, as God has His beady eye on us anyway, whether in our homes or in our church and whether we like it or not. It's all a matter of perception really. And if our home is our church, is it "open all hours", do we welcome the stranger, are our pews available for all?

Where there's a home, there are people. Of course, people don't always get along with each other, least of all families, but in the home of the religious Jew there is a standard set, *shalom bayit*, a peaceful home, that is worth striving for. So *shalom bayit* is important, particularly as the Jewish home is such a hub for the family and community. Its truest expression is defined by the core of every family, that sacred covenant between two people known as marriage. To achieve shalom bayit one needs to achieve domestic bliss, so you've got to get your relationship right with your spouse first. Although the marriage covenant is the starting point, the natural consequence is the building up of a family. The Jewish family unit has been the bedrock of their culture and a key factor to the incredible survival of the Jewish people. While mayhem ruled around and about, this God-ordained unit ticked away doing its stuff, feeding, nurturing and educating the next generation, as we have already seen.

As you enter a religious Jewish home the first thing you notice is the small object affixed to the door post. This is the *mezuzah*, a box containing a scroll. On the scroll are the following verses from the Bible.

Hear, O Israel: The LORD our God, the LORD is one. Love the LORD your God with all your heart and with all your soul and with all your strength. These commandments that I give you today are to be upon your hearts. Impress them on your children. Talk about them when you sit at home and when you walk along the road, when you lie down and when you get up. Tie them as symbols on your hands and bind them on your foreheads. Write them on the doorframes of your houses and on your gates. (Deuteronomy 6:4-9)

This defines everything. It is the *Shema*, the most revered Jewish prayer. It declares the centrality of God and His commandments in this home and the necessity of passing on these beliefs to the children of the household. We saw this earlier when we considered the dining table.

The key concept with *mispocha* is that it is not the nuclear family of 2.4 children that we have been brought up with, but the extended family that includes grandparents, uncles, aunts and cousins, where the cooking pot is in permanent use, where the atmosphere jangles with human voices, cries, prayers and laughter, where caring and sharing crosses the generations. This has become an utterly alien concept to most of us these days. We strive for our own space, we crave personal expression. Community has been replaced by individuality as we disengage our lives from people and replace them with stuff, such as consumer electronics, furniture and objets d'art. Stuff doesn't answer back, stuff doesn't have demands, stuff doesn't need looking after.

But stuff doesn't look after you when you're poorly, stuff doesn't go that extra mile for you, stuff doesn't love you. *Mishpocha* ensures that the wisdom and stories of your grandparents are not lost, *mishpocha* celebrates family occasions as extended times of joy and sharing, *mishpocha* provides an endless supply of babysitters, household operatives and shoulders to cry on. *Mishpocha* means you never need to be lonely, though it could also potentially be stifling and claustrophobic. *Mishpocha*, though, does require a big house.

Mishpocha is most accurately defined as 'the entire family network of relatives by blood or marriage (and sometimes close friends)', so in its widest definition it is talking about a small community, united either by blood or friendship, or in a Christian sense, by conviction (or, in fact, all three). Church families ought to be *mishpocha*, but with that added divine ingredient that ensures relationships are vertical as well as horizontal.

There may be a lot of rethinking needed here for some of us?

Limmud   22

Gerald Crabtree, a geneticist from Stanford University in California, reckons that if an ancient Greek was transported to today, he would be among the cleverest people alive. The reason, he states, is our gradual intellectual decline over the past three thousand years. Certainly, our current culture doesn't encourage people to over-think, with decision making tending to be informed by emotions, public opinion and fear rather than rational thought. Now, what about an ancient Jew, how would he cope in the modern world? It's hard to speculate on his intellectual capacity but one thing is sure is that the scope of his knowledge in one area would be truly outstanding, his knowledge of the *Hebrew Scriptures*.

These days most synagogues have a *'ba'al qoreh'*, an expert at reading Torah scrolls despite the absence of punctuation or vowels. This is chicken-feed compared to the expertise of a six-year old at the time of Jesus, who wouldn't have needed a Torah scroll (and couldn't afford one anyway) but could have recited great big chunks of the Torah from memory, having had it drummed into him from the age of five, starting with Leviticus.

In those days education of schoolkids would have been centred around memorisation of the Hebrew Scriptures and, eventually, the Oral traditions as well. This continued during the diaspora, when children would receive basic education – traditions, scripture and prayer (as well as learning the alphabet at the age of three) - at the family dining table, then they would be shipped off to school at the age of five, where their knowledge of Scripture and Hebrew would be expanded. Remember, we are talking about communities under severe persecution from their "Christian" neighbours, but still maintaining a positive affirming lifestyle. Here's a telling quote from the Mishnah (Menachoth, 99b) that illustrates their position. *"A Rabbi asked 'since I have learnt the whole of Torah may I now study Greek philosophy?',"* the reply came *"'This book of Torah shall not depart out of your mouth but you shall meditate in it day and night (Joshua 1.8)', 'now go and search out at which hour it is neither day nor night and devote it to the study of Greek philosophy'"* As well as memorising Scripture, it was the teachers' responsibility to explain the meanings of the words, in terms of values and the training of behaviour. They were taught the reality of sin and the need to be able to deal with life's challenges, such as the negative behaviour of others. Jewish children would have been taught law, ethics and history, whereas their Gentile contemporaries would have studied science, arts, and linguistics.

When Jesus (or any other contemporary rabbi) hinted at a Scripture in his teachings, the minds of his listeners would *hyperlink* to the correct verses without any need for concordances or computer technology. Even the kids would have Biblical knowledge far surpassing many of our current Christian leaders, though perhaps wouldn't have been quite so hot on the application of the Scripture.

So, here we are, *limmud*, 'study', *the highest form of worship* and, to prove this to you, for the rest of this chapter I will be drawing from an article of the same name by the late great teacher, Dwight Pryor.

Here's a statement made by many a Christian theologian; *"Thirty minutes on your knees in prayer is time better spent than three hours of study in a book."* It seems wise, but is it true? To a Jew at the time of Jesus, this would have been an odd statement to make because, for him, studying Torah was the chief duty and greatest privilege of every Jew. Consider this:

To the Jews who had believed him, Jesus said, "If you hold to my teaching, you are really my disciples. Then you will know the truth, and the truth will set you free." (John 8:31-32)

Also, when asked what was the greatest of all the commandments, his answer was one that any pious Jew would give, *the Shema*, (Deuteronomy 6:4):

He answered, *"'Love the Lord your God with all your heart and with all your soul and with all your strength and with all your mind'; and, 'Love your neighbour as yourself.'"* (Luke 10:27)

Here is the preamble in the Shema: *Hear, O Israel: The LORD our God, the LORD is one*

This is the supreme theological declaration of Judaism and all Biblical faith. It's considered so holy that it's the prayer on the lips of many a Jewish martyr and, when recited in the synagogue, Orthodox Jews cover their eyes with their right hand. It reminds us that the God of Israel is God alone, the Creator of heaven and earth, the one true God.

The **One New Man Bible** translation is closer to the true thoughts behind the words.

Listen! Obey O Israel, the LORD, is our God, the LORD, is One.

It is interesting that the majority of Bibles translate the first word, *shema*, as "hear". But the *One New Man Bible* acknowledges that this word is far more powerful than it seems. It's not a case of just *hearing* but the actions that proceed from that process. It is about *obeying* God, in fact that is another meaning for *shema* elsewhere in Scripture. Hebraic understanding has no truck with just hearing but what effects the Word of God has on you. If you are not moved to action, then you haven't *really* heard.

God's revelation and our recognition of who He really is compels obedience. If knowledge of God is our greatest good, then obedience is our highest virtue, and teaching and study are our essential tasks. So the appropriate response is first to "hear" Him and then to obey Him by teaching His ways (as we saw in the previous chapter). To remind you ...

Love the LORD your God with all your heart and with all your soul and with all your strength. These commandments that I give you today are to be on your hearts. Impress them on your children. Talk about them when you sit at home and when you walk along the road, when you lie down and when you get up. (Deuteronomy 6:5-7)

We are to impress the Lord's revelation upon our own hearts and we are commanded to *"impress them on your children ..."* This was a factor behind God's selection of Abraham:

For I have chosen him, so that he will direct his children and his household after him to keep the way of the LORD by doing what is right and just, so that the LORD will bring about for Abraham what he has promised him (Genesis 18:19).

The Psalms speak eloquently of the great love the Jewish people had for the Torah, the Word of God. The scene is set right at the beginning:

Blessed is the one who does not walk in step with the wicked or stand in the way that sinners take or sit in the company of mockers, but whose delight is in the law of the LORD, and who meditates on his law day and night. (Psalm 1:1-2)

The Jews did not think of Torah as "Law" but instead regarded God as the teacher and Torah was His revelation. It was God's gracious gift of guidance, direction, and instruction, pointing us ever toward life and away from death.

But what of many Gentile Christians today? Is the *shema* their greatest commandment too? What about the 'Great Commission' to evangelise the world? We mustn't forget that Jesus was himself a Jew, a rabbi, who taught Jewish people in the Hebrew language using well-known rabbinic teaching techniques. And his followers, including the Apostles, were all Jews. They did not forsake their Judaism to follow Him; they forsook themselves to embrace Him as the promised Messiah and to follow Him as their Lord. So, with that in mind, let's have a closer look at the 'Great Commission':

Therefore go and make disciples of all nations, baptizing them in the name of the Father and of the Son and of the Holy Spirit, and teaching them to obey everything I have commanded you. And surely I am with you always, to the very end of the age."
(Matthew 28:19-20)

Jesus' emphasis is actually upon learning. *Make disciples*, he implores. A disciple is a learner, a student, one who engages in *limmud*, study. Paul's early rabbi, the great Gamaliel, was noted for having 500 disciples! We too must not only proclaim the good news of the Kingdom of God but also that the converts are taught, in order to become disciples, *teaching them to obey everything I have commanded you*. Teaching and obedience, once again, are inseparable priorities, just like in the *shema*.

Paul was hot on this:

On the first day of the week we came together to break bread. Paul spoke to the people and, because he intended to leave the next day, kept on talking until midnight. There were many lamps in the upstairs room where we were meeting. Seated in a window was a young man named Eutychus, who was sinking into a deep sleep as Paul talked on and on. When he was sound asleep, he fell to the ground from the third story and was picked up dead. Paul went down, threw himself on the young man and put his arms around him. "Don't be alarmed," he said. "He's alive!" Then he went upstairs again and broke bread and ate. After talking until daylight, he left. The people took the young man home alive and were greatly comforted. (Acts 20:7-12)

Because of their intense desire for teaching, he speaks until midnight - a six-hour sermon! Young Eutychus falls asleep in the window and slips to his death three stories below. Then, at Paul's hand his life is renewed and then Paul and the saints immediately return upstairs to get back to business - study. Paul instructs them for another six hours, until daylight! If this was the modern Church one suspects that the narrative would focus on the miracle, with much twittering and facebooking, rather than the continued study. The greater truth is that the teaching of the Lord renews life (Psalm 19:7). It is accompanied by signs and wonders because the Word of God is powerful; properly understood and obeyed, it will never return void but always yields a bountiful harvest.

So we have seen that study, to the Jewish people of Jesus' day, was more than a duty, it was a priceless heritage and an awesome privilege. Before reading the Word of God, the Jew would pray, "*Praise the Lord to whom all praise is due. Praise the Lord to whom all praise is due forever and ever. We praise You, O Lord our God, King of the Universe, Who chose us among all people to reveal to us Your Torah. We praise You, O Lord, Giver of the Torah*." Study, to the Jew, was an act of worship, the highest form of worship. According to one rabbi. "*Greater is the study of the Torah than the rebuilding of the Temple*". (Meg. 16b)

Why the premium upon study? Because it is through the renewing of our minds that we become transformed vessels for true service, fully equipped to do God's Will.

Do not conform to the pattern of this world, but be transformed by the renewing of your mind. Then you will be able to test and approve what God's will is – his good, pleasing and perfect will. (Romans 12:2)

Our minds, therefore, are important. We were created by God with our minds, and as Creator, He wants dominion over them. He commands us to worship Him with our minds, and empowers and quickens our submitted minds to understand the revelation of Himself in His word and in His Word made flesh. And through this renewal process, we are liberated to life, as He promised we would be.

To the Jews who had believed him, Jesus said, "If you hold to my teaching, you are really my disciples. Then you will know the truth, and the truth will set you free." (John 8:31-32)

So, let us return to our earlier question. *Which, then, is better? Thirty minutes of prayer or three hours of study?* This is a very Greek, 'either/or' situation. The Hebrew mind instead declares that both are essential, interrelated, and complementary. Both are expressions of worship. But the worship by the mind must not be neglected or negated. To do so is to deny the clear Biblical witness and to displease our Lord who earnestly desires that we add to our faith, knowledge. And, in the words of Dwight Prior, if we should hear the view that "thirty minutes on your knees in prayer is time better spent than three hours of study," let our response be: "Why not spend three hours *on your knees* in study?!" Amen.

Berakhot 23

We live in an age of short attention spans. This is why twitter reigns supreme as a major means of communication and why the younger generation work on the principle that an emoji speaks a dozen words (or so) 😊

God is not surprised by these developments and, over the years has prompted the Jews to create a compendium of over one hundred blessings, *berakhot*, that can be spoken to God throughout the day. These are short prayers, of a fixed format, that cover a whole range of everyday situations. These *berakhot* are a constant reminder to us of Who we need to bless and acknowledge, first and foremost. When they are a part of our everyday routine, then they function to include God in every situation we find ourselves in. When I say "every", the following examples will illustrate:

"Blessed be the LORD God, King of the Universe, who has created humans with wisdom, with openings and hollow parts, revealed before Your holy throne, that if any part of the body was to malfunction, it would be impossible for us to exist and stand before You even for a short time. You cure all flesh and perform wonders!"

Yes, this is the Jewish prayer for successfully going to the toilet. All in life is a gift from God. Opening ones bowels regularly is a blessing (more so as I get older!).

"I give thanks before You, Living and Eternal King, who has returned within me my soul with compassion; great is Your faithfulness!"

Yes, this is for waking up after sleep and discovering

that you are still alive!

Here's another one. *"Blessed are You, HaShem, our God, King of the Universe, Who has this in His universe."*

This prayer is quite warming. It's what you tell God when you see an exceptionally beautiful person, tree, or field. There's an even more warming variation on this.

*"Blessed are You, **HaShem**, our God, King of the Universe, Who makes the creatures different."*

This is what you tell God when you see exceptionally strange-looking people or animals. You see, to the Jewish eye, everything in this world is of interest to God, not just the "spiritual" stuff. Prayer is meant to be part of life, like eating and drinking, as Rabbi Abraham Heschel reminds us:

"We are trained in maintaining our sense of wonder by uttering a prayer before the enjoyment of food. Each time we are about to drink a glass of water, we remind ourselves of the eternal mystery of creation, "Blessed be Thou ... by Whose word all things come into being." A trivial act and a reference to the supreme miracle. Wishing to eat bread or fruit, to enjoy a pleasant fragrance or a cup of wine; on tasting fruit in season for the first time; on seeing a rainbow, or the ocean; on noticing trees when they blossom; on meeting a sage in Torah or in secular learning; on hearing good or bad tidings– we are taught to invoke His great name and our awareness of Him. Even on performing a physiological function we say "Blessed be Thou ... who healest all flesh and doest wonders." This is one of the goals of the Jewish way of living: to experience commonplace deeds as spiritual adventures, to feel the hidden love and wisdom in all things." (God in Search of Man p. 49).

The general formula is simply to thank God for something. Some of our set prayers tend to miss the simple point expressed here. For instance, think of our grace before meals. When nudged, we sometimes resort to a vague request for God to bless our food. Yet our food is already blessed, it is one of the many gifts that God gives to us. We don't need to *make* the food holy by blessing it. Instead we should be blessing God and thanking Him for His bounty. The idea of blessing the food to make it holy is Greek thinking, from the platonic idea of the separation between the physical and the spiritual, the holy and the profane. Sometimes thinking differently is just thinking Biblically.

Here's the basic formula:

Barukh ata Adonai Eloheinu, melekh ha`olam ...

"Blessed are You, LORD our God, King of the universe ..."

Berakhot come in three basic categories. Firstly, they can be used with pleasurable or key functions, such as eating or drinking, or smelling something nice. When you hold an apple and say, *"Blessed are You, Lord, our God, King of the Universe, who creates the fruit of the tree,"* what you're really saying is this; *Your presence in this world has been made that much greater through this fruit that You created that I am about to enjoy.* It's all about conscious recognition of the Creator and Sustainer, increasing God's presence in the world.

Secondly, you can utter a blessing when performing a good deed, a *mitzvah*, when the following is appended to the basic formula; *"Who has sanctified us through His commandments and has commanded us to ..."*. These deeds include religious obligations, such as lighting candles, reading from the Torah and washing hands.

The final category is times when God is to be praised on special occasions, such as hearing good or bad news, or weather conditions. These are known as "blessings of sight" or "blessings of hearing". The blessing for seeing a rainbow is particularly relevant, as it reminds us of the covenant that God made with Noah:

Whenever I bring clouds over the earth and the rainbow

appears in the clouds, I will remember my covenant between me and you and all living creatures of every kind. Never again will the waters become a flood to destroy all life. Whenever the rainbow appears in the clouds, I will see it and remember the everlasting covenant between God and all living creatures of every kind on the earth."* (Genesis 9:14-16)

As you can see, these three categories cover the whole sweep of our circumstances and, although overuse of such blessings may seem like dry ritual, they are nevertheless appreciated by He who is receiving them, as He is used to being left out of the affairs of man, including by many of us Christians, to our shame. *Mea culpa!*

Although Jewish prayers are taken from their prayer book, the *Siddur*, there's no reason that they can't be added to, or at least the basic form being used to create prayers that we can use in our 21st Century living.

Blessed are You, LORD our God, King of the universe, who has kept my computer virus-free for another day.

One of the most beautiful blessings of all, one that is becoming increasingly adopted by churches, even those outside the Messianic world. It's the Aaronic Blessing.

The LORD bless you and keep you; the LORD make his face shine on you and be gracious to you; the LORD turn his face toward you and give you peace. (Numbers 6:24-26)

God gave this for Aaron, the high priest, to use as the main blessing for the Israelite nation. When the priesthood was disbanded on the loss of the temple, the responsibility for blessing the people passed to the heads of families, the fathers, in the family home, the new temples (*mikdash me'at*), as we have already explored.

When Jesus blessed the children, he placed his hands on them and blessed them (Mark 10:16). In the same way Jewish fathers have blessed their children. Words thus expressed have great power, more so words of Scripture when spoken over one's children.

Here's a simple blessing to get us started.

The blessing of the LORD be on you; I (we) bless you in the name of the Lord. (Psalm 129:8)

How about pausing now, finding someone and praying this blessing over them? Yes, it can be difficult and awkward for some of us, but it's surely a good thing to do despite any brief embarrassment it may give you.

To bless your wife, the model is in Proverbs 31:10-31. According to Jewish tradition, Abraham spoke these words over Sarah. It's a long one, but here's the first few verses:

A wife of noble character who can find? She is worth far more than rubies. Her husband has full confidence in her and lacks nothing of value. She brings him good, not harm, all the days of her life. (Proverbs 31:10-12)

For wives to bless their husbands, we have Psalm 112:1-10. Here is the start:

Praise the LORD. Blessed are those who fear the LORD, who find great delight in his commands. Their children will be mighty in the land; the generation of the upright will be blessed. Wealth and riches are in their houses, and their righteousness endures forever. (Psalm 112:1-3)

The Biblical Jewish tradition of blessing sons is for the father to lay his hands on the son's head and recite the Aaronic blessing:

The LORD bless you and keep you; the LORD make his face shine on you and be gracious to you; the LORD turn his face toward you and give you peace. (Numbers 6:24-26)

This can be followed by personal blessings in the same manner as Jacob blessed his twelve sons individually (Genesis 49:28). You may also want to add something like this:

"May your mouth speak with wisdom. May your heart

meditate with reverence. May your hands do the work that God has given you. May your feet hasten to follow the path that God has laid out for your life".

Daughters are blessed in the way that Ruth was blessed in Ruth 4:11:

"May the LORD make the woman who is coming into your home like Rachel and Leah, who together built up the family of Israel."

Again this should be followed by personal blessings, expressing your desires for your daughter's happiness and success. You may also want to add something like this:

"Blessed are you of the Lord, my daughter, for you have been kind and generous. The Lord God is your God and His people are your people. May all the people know of certainty that you are a virtuous daughter".

Then there are blessings for special occasions, for instance at mealtimes. Although most Christians say their blessing ("grace before meal") before the meal, the Biblical precedent is to pray after you have eaten. This is the *Birkath HaMazon*, the oldest blessing of all.

When you have eaten and are satisfied, praise the LORD your God for the good land he has given you. (Deuteronomy 8:10)

We are all to bless each other. God blesses us through His grace, then we bless others not just through our words but also our actions, the spiritual gifts that He freely gives to us for the express purpose of ... blessing others. But we must also bless God Himself through thanksgiving. Thus it is a circle of blessing – from God to man and back to God - and we are all a part of it. Who have you blessed today? Who have I blessed today?

What did the Gentiles ever do for us?

24

Today the Lord woke me up at 6am. What followed was a consolidation in my mind of various strands regarding Gentiles, that needed tying together, some of which had been flapping around, all sad and lonely, for quite some time. It all came together this morning as I had already planned to think more about Gentiles, for the purposes of this chapter. God really does work in weird and wonderful ways.

I am going to start with what may seem to be a rant, but in fact is just a shrewd observance. The trigger was a post I uploaded into the weekly blog I do for Premier Radio, **Yeshua Explored**. I have been adding these for nearly seven years and have produced well over five hundred such posts. Despite little promotion, these are reasonably popular and particularly so on Facebook, where I post links to a number of relevant user groups. One such group, frequented by fellow Christian writers has bucked this trend and has been a graveyard of indifference to my work ... until yesterday. The title of my post was *Christians who hate the Jews*. It hit a raw nerve and suddenly there was activity, with much bluster and denial, of the *'I've never spoken or heard a word of anti-Semitism in my church, not once'* variety. I seemed to have killed the debate dead with my observation that it is deeds not words that we need to focus on, particularly 'sins of omission' rather than 'sins of commission'. What did I mean by this?

For the past twenty years or so I have occasionally run small stands at Christian exhibitions, such as the *Christian*

Resources Exhibition, at Esher. Each time was in the forlorn hope that *this time people will take notice and engage with me, even if just to criticise*. No such hope, such interactions, in total, I can count on the fingers of my hands. Even more tragically, I have also exhibited for the past seven or eight years at the annual *Christian Retailers Retreat*, where the great and the good of the Christian publishing industry come together, from distributors and bookshops to authors and publishers. One ministry that has always exhibited nearby is the very same ministry that runs the Facebook user group mentioned earlier. The stand was occupied by a procession of authors on a rota system, mostly middle aged white lady novelists. This year they were directly opposite me, they couldn't fail to notice me. *Here was the awkward Jewish fellow who has posted 568 times in our Facebook group, every week for nearly seven years. We know it is him because his name is all over the books that are displayed on his table just two metres away from us. Perhaps we should acknowledge him?*

Unfortunately, this was another forlorn hope on my part as not once has any of my fellow authors approached me either this year, or any other year, if only to say, *I've seen your posts and I love them / hate them / am not sure about them"*. Not one. I might as well inhabit a different universe. The same goes for over 90% of my fellow publishers, authors as well as distributors and shops. Yes, I'm not the most outgoing of souls and "marketing" is certainly not my middle name, but surely this can't be right? It isn't right and it's just another symptom of the problem that One New Man, along with anything about the Jews in a "future" sense is ignored, with Ephesians 2 joining Romans 11 and Jeremiah 31 as inconvenient blind spots, consigned to the periphery if not further.

In my earlier years this filled me with anger and drove

me into cynical thought patterns that did nobody any good and I thank God for my editors who squeeze my manuscripts dry of such outbursts before the final book hits the shelf (before bouncing back into the waste paper basket – whoops, you missed that one!) Now I just feel sorry for the wider Church, to which I feel called in a teaching capacity. If only I could get them to listen to me, or read my books! I really think that, until we have a true *One New Man* with Jew and Gentile in honest and productive unity, the Body of Christ is not functioning on all cylinders. Which brings me to the heading of this chapter.

What did the Gentiles ever do for us?

Of course this is just a wordplay on the intentionally ironic question posed in the Monty Python film, "Life of Brian" (not recommended, of course). The point is that the Romans did actually do quite a lot, a fact only grudgingly accepted. It seems from conversations had with many Messianic believers, particularly Gentiles, that the Gentile Church has blown it, particularly in its historic treatment of the Jews and its readiness to create its own traditions, born out of Greek thinking. Mostly true, but let's not throw out the baby with the bathwater, because the Gentiles have given us something most precious ... *the Church itself.*

Before we explore this, let's recap on what the Jews could have given us if only they had been given the chance:

- **Sabbath** (*Shabbat*)
  A Biblical injunction for restorative rest with God and family, in accordance with your personal leading and circumstances.
- **Passover** (*Pesach*) and the festivals.
  Biblical feasts that teach us in a family setting about

God and His ways.
- **Joy** (*Simcha*)
  The joy that comes from community living and shared lives.
- **Life** (*Chaim*)
  Worshipping God in dance and music that energise the soul and body and lift the spirit.
- **Holiness** (*Kadosh*)
  Understanding the Holiness of God and taking this seriously in all aspects of your daily life.
- *Chesed*
  Understanding that much about God is mysterious but realising that His very nature is to go above and beyond the expected.
- **Family** (*Mishpochah*)
  Realising the importance of the family home in teaching the next generation and preparing them for life.
- **Study** (*Limmud*)
  Realising the importance of knowledge and the study needed to gain an understanding of the important things in life.
- **Blessings** (*Berachot*)
  Sharing every aspect of your life with God by blessing Him and thanking Him for all that He has given you.

Of course, you will look through this list and tick boxes where some of these aspects are realities in your life. That is to be commended and it's not just that the Jews have a monopoly in these areas, it's just that, through their precarious and uncertain existence over the last 2,000 years, they have done their best to live lives in the way of their fathers, and the fathers before them and so on. There are other aspects of Jewish life that are not so hot as no-one can claim to be perfect, just in case you accuse me of unnecessary eulogising. But it is important to emphasise the positive and make an effort to learn from the experience of others.

So now we return to our question, *what have the Gentiles done for us* and ponder the answer that I suggested. The biggest thing we can thank the Gentiles for is the preservation of the *true* Church. Of course, I am not referring to the corruption known as *Christendom*, driven by greed, power, lust and violence that has blighted mainstream Church history and has given us such aberrations as the Crusades, the Inquisition, "Christian" anti-Semitism, "holy" wars, persecution of other Christians, "divine right of Kings", slavery, bad attitude towards women and minority groups and so on. Running parallel to this and on the margins is what has been termed the "remnant" Church. Here are some glimpses of their story (the full account is in my book **To Life**):

There's a tiny island called Iona, off the coast of Scotland. It was one of the first places in the whole of these British Isles to really experience authentic Biblical Christianity, which spread throughout Scotland. One man brought this Gospel, this Good News untainted by the *Greek* additions, to Iona. He was an Irishman called Columba, who arrived in AD 563 and established a Christian community that was very different from what was becoming the norm in Europe in the 6th Century AD, as it entered the *Dark Ages*. He had already planted forty one similar communities in Ireland, but none of them would have such far-reaching influence as this one on Iona.

Here was real community, under the benevolent direction of the Abbot, of whom Columba was the first. Members of this community were allowed to marry, unlike their counterparts on mainland Europe. They were extremely Bible literate and were taught to memorise whole passages of Scripture. They also only baptised those who professed faith and celebrated the death and resurrection of Jesus according to the Hebrew calendar. From this base a relentless period of evangelism was launched, leading to the creating of around sixty similar communities in Scotland before Columba's death. But the arrival of Augustine to these shores, within a year of Columba's death, was to signal the beginning of the end of this independent expression of the Christian faith and Britain was eventually sucked into the paganised Roman Catholic system. So what happened to the pure faith of the apostles in the meantime? There surely had to be a surviving remnant somewhere?

Any group that defied the various State churches tended to be denounced as heretics and their written material burned. So it is difficult to find an impartial historical witness for any expression of Christianity other than the Greek-tainted party-line of official Christendom. A good place to start is to investigate the groups that were hunted, denounced, persecuted and tortured at the hands of the Inquisition or the early Crusades. If they came to the attention of the Popes, the chances were that they were promoting a "different Gospel" to the corrupted version that had been synthesised by the philosophers and theologians and fed to the masses. This made them worthy of investigation.

One such group was the *Waldenses*. This group lived in the valleys of the alpine regions of Northern Italy. They may have shared a country with the Roman Catholics, but they couldn't have been more different. They had a high view of Holy Scripture, it was their rule of life, it was a living book for them. They firmly believed in preaching and were very good at it, even counting many Catholics among their converts. They also firmly believed that the Pope was not God's representative on earth and offered allegiance to Jesus Christ alone.

Another unbroken link from the 1st Century were the *Paulicians*, who took their name from the Apostle Paul and first appeared in Antioch, where Barnabas and Paul preached and where believers were first called *Christians* and where many Jewish Christians migrated after being forced out of Jerusalem. These first Christians were able to migrate northwards to Armenia before the Greek pagan influences took hold. They were resolute in holding firm to the true faith and spoke up against what they saw as unbiblical practices, such as the veneration of relics, the worship of Mary and the saints and the excesses surrounding the Catholic Mass.

But now back to England. It is the 14th Century and a remarkable man steps onto the stage. This is John Wycliffe, the man who had both the cheek and the grace to translate the Bible from the Latin into English, something unheard of in the Catholic world, where the clear words of Scripture were hidden from the common man. As a result of this, he made a remarkable discovery that was to revolutionise the Christian faith and start a process that led to the sweeping changes of the Reformation many years later. His discovery was ....*the Word of God*. Through translating the Bible into English its very words began to grip his soul and others who followed him. These were the *Lollards*, a derisive name (the 'babblers') given to them by others, a movement labelled a heresy by the Pope and also resisted in this country by the Archbishop of Canterbury. It resulted in the first execution of a layman in England as a heretic; that was John Badby in the 15th Century.

A man called Jerome had listened intently to Wycliffe's

sermons in Oxford and took the message of reform for the Catholic Church back to his home city of Prague, in Central Europe. He in turn was listened to by John Huss, a man already influenced by the Waldenses and a new movement was born, the *Hussites*. Huss was immediately excommunicated by the Pope, who also publicly burned Wycliffe's writings, then a few years later, both Jerome and Huss were burned at the stake. This was serious business, indeed.

Around fifty years after John Huss's death a group of his followers, the Bohemian Brethren, morphed into the *Moravians*, one of the first true Protestant Churches. In the early 18th Century, under the leadership of the German nobleman, Count Zinzendorf, they had an encounter with God. On August 13th 1727 the Holy Spirit came down on a group of them with such power that, according to one of them, *"we hardly knew whether we belonged to earth or had already gone to Heaven."* It was a revival. Out of this came the following: A 24/7 prayer initiative that lasted 100 years, the first ever publication of a daily devotional, the planting of 30 churches, the formation of hundreds of "house churches" and the first ever Protestant mission movement, sending out hundreds of missionaries all over the world.

In 1738, one such missionary, Peter Boehler, had a meeting in London with one John Wesley, informing him that what he needed was true saving faith. Three months later, during a meeting in Aldersgate Street, Wesley relates, *"I felt my heart strangely warmed. I felt I did trust in Christ, Christ alone for salvation, and an assurance was given me that he had taken away my sins, even mine, and saved me from the law of sin and death."*

Thus was born *Methodism*, that started out as a major revival within the Church of England, before becoming a denomination of its own. It is perhaps safe to say that this was the first time the visible and the invisible churches crossed paths, without bloodshed. The Church of England, a dissident branch of the established Western Church with its roots in Rome and the ideas of the Greek philosophers had collided with the fruit of the long history of the dissident Church, from the Paulicians and Waldenses through to the Lollards, Hussites and Moravians. And the result was ... revival! England and the USA were transformed by the Methodists, who took God to the people, with their relentless open-air preaching. They transformed society from the bottom up.

The Methodists were very disciplined in their religious life and practices, with an emphasis on personal holiness, living the life that they preached (which has not always been the case with Christians). They had regular private devotions and met daily for prayer and Bible study. Eventually they organised themselves into regional groups, stressing discipleship, fellowship and pastoral care. Eventually they split from the Anglicans and became a worldwide movement, still active today, albeit without the doctrinal purity of those early days.

I think my point has been made. Church history is not just about the main stories, the familiar stories promoted by the Catholics and the Protestants and the conflicts between them. Such has been the visible Church, the one with the ear of the historians. But, as I have shown, there has been a second, "alternative" Church in Europe, living in the margins, often hidden out of fear of persecution, but a Church without which the Reformation may never have happened. This is the Church largely unsullied by Greek philosophy. I have presented just a flavour of their activities and importance and, of course this has not been an unbroken line, though it was interesting to trace a path from Wycliffe in Oxford to Wesley in London, by way of Prague, Bohemia and Moravia.

We stand on the shoulders of such giants and we must thank the *Gentile Church of the remnant* that has brought the Gospel to the current day, often surviving on the fringes and often at odds with the established Church on matters of doctrinal purity, trustworthiness of the Bible and the unchanging character of God.

This is what the Gentiles have given us.

Any reading of "religious" history would marvel not just at the survival of the Jewish people against all odds, but also of the remnant Church. Yet both have survived, intact ... but still apart.

Gentiles have been grafted into the Olive tree of Romans 11, unnatural branches alongside the natural branches of the Jews and both nourished from the Hebraic roots. The tree has survived to modern times, battered and with predominantly unnatural Gentile branches.

Israel has experienced a hardening in part until the full number of the Gentiles has come in. (Romans 11:25)

Is it a huge jump to believe that we may now have reached this point and God wants to restore this tree according to original intentions? If this is true, we should be seeing more and more Jews being welcomed into the Kingdom. If so, how will they be received by the Church? The track record is not a good one. Could *One New Man* be the solution, a safe, welcoming place where Jews and Gentiles can share a common destiny, but through celebrating their uniqueness?

Doesn't it also say:

For if their rejection brought reconciliation to the world, what will their acceptance be but life from the dead? (Romans 11:15)

Could life from the dead refer to bringing back *chaim*

into the Church, as well as *simcha, kadosh, chesed, mishpocha, limmud* and *berachot*? How wonderful would that be?

And this is why *One New Man* must be initiated as an initiative of the Gentile Church. To repeat what I said in an earlier chapter, if you re-read Ephesians 2 you realise that Paul places the initiative at the feet of the Gentiles.

So, on the one hand we have the Gentile remnant Church, comprising of Bible believers who believe in the full counsel of God in every way, including a desire to see the fruition of Ephesians 2. And, on the other hand, we have Messianic believers in Jesus, both Jew and Gentile, who are eager for the Church to rediscover the true roots of the faith.

Could a merger be in the offing, even on a small scale?

How this is to happen is primarily down to the Will and timing of Almighty God. Are we willing to be agents of reconciliation and unity? Could One New Man become a reality? A true *shalom of oneness?*

Finding Oneness 25

In terms of the relationship between Jew and Gentile, we have identified two key passages of Scripture. We have the One New Man of Ephesians 2, of course, but we also have the warnings to the Gentiles given in Romans 11. Taking the two together and using the tools of form and function I believe we can formulate a pretty good summary and way forwards in our search for 'Oneness'.

We start off with the *form*. What is the form of a Jew and a Gentile? Who is a Jew and who is a Gentile? Paul gives us a good clue in Ephesians:

Therefore, remember that formerly you who are Gentiles by birth and called "uncircumcised" by those who call themselves "the circumcision" (which is done in the body by human hands). (Ephesians 2:11)

The Jews are the circumcised ones, the ones with the physical mark. It is a physical indicator, not something that is chosen or spiritualised or imagined or even hoped for. Ironically the Nazis got right to the point with the *Nuremberg Laws,* forbidding 'impure' relations between Jews and Germans. For them a Jew is someone with three or four Jewish grandparents, it was purely a matter of blood not religion. So should it be for us, a bloodline, just like the one that connected Jesus to his forbears. This makes it easy for us to decide who is a Gentile … *everybody else who isn't a Jew.*

Oh, if it were only this straightforward for some. It is beyond irony to realise that despite Jewish people being those most hated, reviled and persecuted in history, there are some who even wish to hijack their very identity. This is *identity politics* – something I spoke about in detail in *Into the Lion's Den* – gone mad. There is a current trend for whole swathes of humanity to define themselves according to a form defined by others, an aspect of their origin or behaviour or lifestyle, groupings usually allied to culture, race, gender or religion. This is often to the detriment of any function that God may have for them, which helps us to understand the anti-God origins of the process.

Unfortunately, this has spread to some aspects of the Church. Historically we have the anathema of Replacement Theology, taking many forms, and asserting that the Gentile Church is the 'New Israel' (This is comprehensively refuted in *Outcast Nation*), thus stripping away any spiritual identity Jewish people may have in God's purposes and rendering 'null and void' many of the cast-iron promises that God gave the Jews in the Old Testament, such as in Jeremiah 31:35-37:

This is what the LORD says, he who appoints the sun to shine by day, who decrees the moon and stars to shine by night, who stirs up the sea so that its waves roar– the LORD Almighty is his name: "Only if these decrees vanish from my sight," declares the LORD, "will Israel ever cease being a nation before me." This is what the LORD says: "Only if the heavens above can be measured and the foundations of the earth below be searched out will I reject all the descendants of Israel because of all they have done," declares the LORD.

But there is also a more sinister aspect of this. There are "Christian" groups who assert that many modern Jews aren't even physical Jews, but imposters, descendants of Gentile tribes living in Russia many centuries ago. This is a thoroughly discredited theory but convenient in feeding an anti-Semitic narrative. It allows the 'British Israelites', 'Black Hebrews' and various revisionists to make claims to being the 'true Jews', in order to bolster their own sense of "identity", even if there are no solid facts to back them up. This is all part of the post-modern "believe what you like" world that we currently live in! Of course, if the neo-Nazis ever came to power, these movements would disappear like a flash and drop their *faux Yiddishkeit* like a ton of bricks!

So a Jew is a Jew and a Gentile is a Gentile. Now for the *function*. This is where it gets interesting and where we broaden our outlook, looking at individual Jews and Gentiles, but also at the Jewish and Gentile people as a whole.

As individuals it is easy, but often misunderstood. The clue is in Galatians:

There is neither Jew nor Gentile, neither slave nor free, nor is there male and female, for you are all one in Christ Jesus. (Galatians 3:28)

For an individual, in terms of your salvation and your place in God's purposes, we are all the same, there is no difference in Jew or Gentile. We all share in the same function:

*And we all, who with unveiled faces contemplate the Lord's glory, are **being transformed into his image** with ever-increasing glory, which comes from the Lord, who is the Spirit.* (2 Corinthians 3:18)

Our function as Christians is to be transformed into the image and likeness of Jesus, our model. Does this also mean that, in Christ, our form is not fixed, with our goal to achieve the form of Jesus himself? No, we need to think about form in a physical sense. We are physically and biologically either Jew or Gentile and although we wish to be transformed into the image and likeness of Jesus, this is not a physical transformation, but a functional change, through the process of sanctification.

There is only one rider to this, a controversial one and a mystery to all, save God Himself. In terms of the impact that individual Jews have made on our world – for good and for bad – *there is something going on there.* Perhaps it is an outworking of God's blessings to Abraham (Genesis 12 etc.), or perhaps it can be explained in other terms, the fact is that ... it is a fact. It has been estimated that 22% of all Nobel Prize winners in the 20th Century were Jewish, a people who comprise just 0.19% of the population! There is definitely something going on here!

It's when we look at people groups that the perspective changes. In terms of the Jewish people as a whole, we have already looked at what they could offer the Church, in those eight Hebrew words; *moedim, chaim, simcha, berachot, limmud, mishpachah, kadosh* and *chesed*. Romans 11 provides an emphasis, that perhaps alludes to this:

But if their transgression means riches for the world, and their loss means riches for the Gentiles, how much greater riches will their full inclusion bring! (Romans 11:12)

For if their rejection brought reconciliation to the world, what will their acceptance be but life from the dead? (Romans 11:15)

Life from the dead! A promise of *chaim* ... and the rest? We also looked at Gentiles and asked, *what did they bring to the table?* And the answer was perhaps unexpected. They have, in the form of the remnant, those who have stuck to Biblical principles and have refused to be drawn into the ways of the world, given us *the Church itself.*

But again, there's a rider, one spelled out in Romans 11.

Do not consider yourself to be superior to those other branches. If you do, consider this: You do not support the root, but the root supports you. (Romans 11:18)

Do not be arrogant, but tremble. For if God did not spare the natural branches, he will not spare you either. (Romans 11:20,21)

It's a warning to Gentiles that fell on deaf ears mostly. It is virtually a prophecy and God knew that Gentiles would fail here, that they would, in their arrogance, act against the natural branches, the Jews. I don't see much trembling, perhaps there's still a judgement coming on the Church? However you view this, perhaps the Gentile Church still has a function to perform here? Those who have preserved the remnant Church largely have a good track record regarding their Jewish brethren, but perhaps there is more they can do to educate the rest of the Church and bring it to acknowledgement and repentance on the heinous crimes of their forebears and perhaps their current indifference (and maybe worse).

It has always been a puzzle for me that *One New Man* never seemed to find true fulfilment in history. The first generation of believers were Jewish and a critical issue that arose was *'what to do with these Gentiles'?* Once basic methodologies were established by the Jerusalem Council in Acts 15, Gentiles began trickling, then flooding into the Church. Then we move into post-Biblical history, where there is an initial silence, followed by reports of an established Church run by the Gentile Church Fathers in the 2nd Century onwards, with every intent of purging all Jewishness from their thoughts and practices. Where was *One New Man* all this time? Did it flourish briefly during those silent years of transition ... or had it not happened at all? It appears that, after that first generation, the Jewish and Gentile believers began to move apart, even physically, especially since the Jews flew to Pella in the east, when the Romans sacked Jerusalem in AD70. From that point onwards, sadly, the Jews exit stage left for the remainder of the performance that was Church history. The Diaspora, the *Galut*, became a spiritual one as well as a physical one.

Does this mean that Paul, in Ephesians 2, was writing specifically about a fulfilment that may only just be flickering into existence a full 2,000 years later?

I decided to revisit the letter to the Ephesians, but I decided on a different approach, to see if I could gain extra insights. I created a visual representation of the letter, using Powerpoint, to the accompaniment of the David Suchet NIV audio commentary (Hodder and Stoughton audiobook). You can see it at: https://www.youtube.com/watch?v=LcjF2KOUKvA&t=748s

In this presentation I cut back on some of Paul's flowery and devotional language and instead concentrated on the key concepts being developed. The story that began to unfold was that in the context of God's masterplan to bring unity to His creation (Ephesians 1:9-10), the major thrust was God's own answer to that question, 'what to do with these Gentiles'? The Jews were a given, they were the *near* people, the natural branches and the natural inheritors of the promise. God's intentions were wrapped up in the mystery of the Gentiles (Ephesians 3:6), how the *far* people, the unnatural branches can be grafted in as an equal partner in the 'Grand Undertaking' of the Body of Christ, the great temple of believers.

Most Gentiles probably don't understand what a privilege they have been granted, yet they must have known that right at the beginning, when Paul was first revealing his revelation. Yet how quickly this went sour and the Gentile Church was eventually responsible for creating a "Church of Unnatural Branches", *Christendom,* the power structures that have dominated most of Church history. They have made a mockery out of a mystery and surely the promises of those chapters are still yet to be fulfilled, when

Jew and Gentile can truly be reconciled in unity:

His intent was that now, through the church, the manifold wisdom of God should be made known to the rulers and authorities in the heavenly realms, according to his eternal purpose that he accomplished in Christ Jesus our Lord. In him and through faith in him we may approach God with freedom and confidence. (Ephesians 3:10-12)

This is a major declaration and speaks of a time when even the demonic world is going to sit up and notice, because it is going to see a Church in true unity, characterised by the oneness of the One New Man, of Jew and Gentile. This, I believe, is still in the future, but, perhaps a future fast approaching.

If these things can begin to happen then I believe we can finally see a shalom of Oneness emerging in God's Church and a loud message proclaimed *to the rulers and authorities in the heavenly realms*. The message is this: *watch out, we have finally got our act together!*

PART FIVE
The Shalom of Shaloms

It happened in Devon   26

Here's a chapter I never intended to write because it references a series of events that came *after* the writing of the first draft of this book. Also, as it is discussing ideas put forwards in the previous section on the 'One New Man', it is actually in the wrong section. But this doesn't bother me, as *this thing is bigger than mere literary conventions*. Last week, at our Foundations 10 "conference" (for want of a better word) in Sidholme Hotel, Devon, my last few chapters – where I describe the seven things that the Church has lost since it threw out its Hebrew roots – *came alive!*

First, *simcha*, joy. Let us remind ourselves what the Psalms often tell us to do:

Rejoice in the LORD and be glad, you righteous; sing, all you who are upright in heart! (Psalm 32:11)

Worship is mostly associated with music and is often initiated by the activating of a play-list within the control of a *worship leader*. We had worship leaders, but none of them had a play-list, neither did any of them sing or play a musical instrument. Our worship leaders were chosen as mature believers who could lead us into the heart of God and His needs, which doesn't always require the twanging of guitar strings. Of course, music is an important component but it's not the be-all-and-end-all. Nevertheless, we also had a small worship group to play mostly up-tempo Messianic songs and two keyboard players to lead us into some more traditional hymns. But it is fair to say that most singing was *acapella*, unaccompanied human voices, powerful, raw and often most joyful. This joy was released when a single voice from within the "congregation" bravely cut into the silence, worship initiated by an individual prompted by the Holy Spirit and always joined by others.

Then there was *chaim*, life. Life can be messy and unstructured, which is also how we like to do Foundations. Schedules are overwritten, workshops clash and people are encouraged either to pack in the wide variety of workshops on offer ... or just to do nothing. Life should be about challenges.

The thief comes only to steal and kill and destroy; I have come that they may have life, and have it to the full. (John 10:10)

Too often Christian gatherings are lifeless and predictable, yet Jesus came to bring us *life to the full*. For real *shalom* we need to cater for all of our individual needs, mind, body and spirit. Sometimes we miss out on so much because we Christians are not stretched and encouraged to try out something new. One such challenge is dance, a wonderful expression of *chaim*. Near the beginning of the week, Robert, one of the *Sh'ma Kingdom dancers* made a plea for men to burst through their reticence and 'fear of looking daft' and join the dance workshop. To be frank, this is evidently a work in progress and not too many took the challenge, yet we ended up with a dance team of around twenty people, including some young children, who performed a three part dance/drama routine on the Friday, a lot of it centred on a song written by our Messianic worship leader, David Macrow, based on my book, *Into the Lion's Den* and acted out with swords and much exuberance, accompanied by a twenty-piece choir trained from scratch by David and his bouncy wife, Keila. It was life and joy all wrapped up in one fifteen-minute sequence and available for all to see on YouTube.

Kadosh, holiness, tends to be overlooked in our

busyness. It speaks of separation, away from the noise of our world and its concerns. We felt very much that we were in a holy place, trapped together within the four walls (actually quite a lot of walls) of the hotel and aligning us together in thinking about things of God.

... *be holy, because I am holy.* (Leviticus 11:45)

Kadosh was in the silences between the songs, in the shared craft activities, in those moments when the penny dropped and clarity filled the mind during a teaching session, in the private and corporate times when individuals were prayed over. It was also in the streets when our evangelists hit the town and brought a touch of heaven to people who had long lost any ideas of true hope in a Saviour. *Kadosh* lived when the self died and the focus was on God and His ways.

Then there was that wonderful, complex-yet-simple word, *chesed*, going beyond what is expected. God's chesed was wonderfully reflected that week in the actions of His people. There were undoubtedly many stories of *chesed* in Sidholme; some will be told, some will remain private.

By this everyone will know that you are my disciples, if you love one another." (John 13:35)

Here are just three of them.

We made a decision as a leadership team to bring what we saw as a grave injustice to light. It concerned a beloved brother who has been relentlessly persecuted over the last few years by fellow Christians in the local church and in the Messianic world, through a campaign of gossip and rejection. In his earlier life he had given in to homosexual impulses, but had woken up, repented of this and put his past behind him. Unfortunately, others have chosen to judge him, have rejected him rather than seeking to understand him and have obstructed him in his ministry, despite his undoubted gifts as a communicator, organiser and evangelist. At Foundations we gave him the chance to publicly tell his story, right at the beginning of the week. It was a risk as the conference could have had its path deflected. But God blessed this endeavour and our brother was showered with love and acceptance all week and left us as a changed man.

A brother made a decision to give up much of his free time at Foundations in order to mentor two people through the fascinating activity of spoon making – creating a wooden spoon from a lump of wood, a process that took six or seven hours. He brought all of his tools along – including a set of axes and carving knives – and guided two people through this process. It was, for all three of them, a time of great blessing and fellowship.

During the Prophetic Art workshop, Rosie instructed people on how to create cards that could be used to bless people. These cards were given out during the outreach but also, at the end of the week, many people received cards with a specific message just for them. One elderly gentleman was such a recipient, given a sealed card by a young lady and asked not to read it until he returned home. When he did read it, the message spoke directly into his heart and his life would be significantly impacted.

Mishpocha, family, was probably the abiding theme of the week. It was the word that was spoken more than any other in testimony times in the conference room and in the assessment forms and in emails since the event. Foundations 10 was basically a *family outing*, with the newcomers, numbering around a third of the delegates, grafted in to a growing national family. We were a mixture of young and old, from the one year old, Elijah Stevenson to a whole gaggle of sprightly octogenarians. Each belonged to each other, cared for each other, prayed for each other. It was that sort of event. Church is meant to be family after all, as we have already seen, in the passage that leads on directly after the One New Man revelation:

Consequently, you are no longer foreigners and strangers, but fellow citizens with God's people and also members of his household. (Ephesians 2:19)

It's one thing nodding away in agreement at a heartening Bible passage, *but a very different thing to actually live it out*. The reason why a church family emerged so quickly and effectively was because we had created a safe place, a place of trust and acceptance. We rejected any hierarchical approach, any clergy/laity divide, with a team of helpers comprised of almost a half of the able-bodies available and with an ethos that encouraged everybody to make some sort of contribution, however small, whether a prayer, a story, a testimony (even our nine year olds gave their assessments of the week) a piece of art, a willing voice, through dance, drama, music, crafts or one of our immensely popular ten minute *show & tells*, where we heard of angelic encounters, stories from a taxi cab, unlikely evangelistic opportunities and the Von Trapp-Stevenson clan (all seven and a half of them) singing a song to bless us all, particularly the children.

Limmud, study, has always been a major part of Foundations. In some earlier conferences we packed in end-to-end teaching sessions, as seems to be the norm on the conference circuit, with scarcely room to breathe, let alone assimilate the wisdom being offered. Now we go for quality, rather than quantity. It's not necessarily that our teachers are of a higher calibre, as we have tended to use the same teachers from conference to conference. But less can often be more:

Do your best to present yourself to God as one approved, a worker who does not need to be ashamed and who correctly handles the word of truth. (2 Timothy 2:15)

To really handle the word of truth sometimes we must allow it to marinate within us and this can only effectively happen if we give it time to do so. So, at Foundations 10, we cut back on teaching slots to just two or three key messages a day and each was usually followed by a *yeshiva*, a prolonged time of questioning and discussion, to make sure the message holds and is remembered ... and acted on. We were greatly encouraged to find that the messages given seemed to dovetail into each other in terms of themes and even Scriptures referenced, although the teachers each prepared their lessons in isolation!

And, finally, we have *berachot*, blessings. Paul Luckraft actually taught on this subject early on in the week as we wanted it to be a persistent theme and a practical exercise.

Whoever brings blessing will be enriched, and one who waters will himself be watered. (Proverbs 11:25 ESV)

We all consciously went out of our way to speak blessings to each other, often just a few words and, as mentioned before, many cards passed hands, for that very purpose. And, at the very end, Keila pronounced the Aaronic blessing to all of us, in Hebrew and in English. A fitting end to a blessed time for all (spoken from right to left).

	v'yishmerecha	*Adonai y'varekecha*
	and He will keep you	The LORD will bless you
	eleycha panav	*Adonai ya'er*
	upon you His face	The LORD will shine
	panav Adonai yisa	*vichunecha*
	The LORD lift up His countenance	be gracious to you
	shalom lecha	*v'yasem eleycha*
	shalom to you	and establish to you

These are not just my observations. Here is a poem, written afterwards by one of the delegates:

Bonded together is one unity; how precious, how sweet, together to be!

Words are inadequate to describe the sublime but here is a flavour of our happy time:

The teaching was centred on God's Word not man's, we were exhorted to surrender to Father's plans.

To lay down our rebellion and come out of the dark and heed the LORD's call to join Him in the ark.

To rid ourselves of the fear of man; instead fearing Him Who ultimately can.

Throw body and soul to the fires of hell; not shrinking, not compromising, a gospel to tell.

From our advantage in Jesus far above, we can soar over trouble on wings of a dove.

And fix our eyes on our glory, our crown; keep standing in victory and keep looking down!

There was dancing in freedom, arts and crafts, timelines, evangelism and quite a few laughs!

Yeshivas, cartoons, we could show and could tell, with preaching umpired by a heresy bell.

True repentance that washes and cleanses the soul, was aided and abetted by a large fish bowl.

A man in white made a courageous stand; his garments cleansed by the blood of the Lamb.

The blessing of children, what a joy to behold; sweetness of fellowship for the young and the old.

Words won't suffice for adequately expressing, the fellowship, joy and wonderful blessing.

All we can do is simply lay at His feet, those costly sins that His blood did defeat.

We give God all the glory, our voices we raise, our hearts full of wonder, love and praise.

So, this chapter may seem self-indulgent but it was a chapter begging to be written while the events of the past week are still fresh in my mind. I sincerely believe that God gave us a tiny glimpse into possibilities. Could this have been a key to real Christian living? Could *One New Man* be a bigger, more important, concept than we had ever imagined it to be?

I think this may well be so, in fact it's time we returned to Holy Scripture, to the passages that speak most clearly about this ...

The Shalom of shaloms   27

It recently occurred to me that this book is a simplified commentary of the first three chapters in the Book of Ephesians. Perhaps now is a good time to read those passages in their entirety before we move on. The first chapter reveals to us the glorious reality of our salvation, we have entered into the *shalom of salvation*, by royal command, by imperial decree, by the mysterious outworking of grace, that rewarder of the unworthy!

For he chose us in him before the creation of the world (vs 4)
He predestined us for adoption to sonship through Jesus Christ (vs 5)
In him we were also chosen (vs 11)
When you believed, you were marked in him with a seal, the promised Holy Spirit (vs 13)
I pray that the eyes of your heart may be enlightened in order that you may know the hope to which he has called you, the riches of his glorious inheritance in his holy people (vs 18)

But there's more, there has to be a purpose to this. Paul describes this in verses 8-10:

With all wisdom and understanding, he made known to us the mystery of his will according to his good pleasure, which he purposed in Christ, to be put into effect when the times reach their fulfillment—to bring unity to all things in heaven and on earth under Christ.

To bring unity to all things in heaven and on earth under Christ. The function of all functions, God's grand purpose! God's masterplan!

And how does He do this? *The shalom of unity.* We are

not a collection of random islands, there is something that connects us horizontally, as well as vertically.

Consequently, you are no longer foreigners and strangers, but fellow citizens with God's people and also members of his household, built on the foundation of the apostles and prophets, with Christ Jesus himself as the chief cornerstone. In him the whole building is joined together and rises to become a holy temple in the Lord. And in him you too are being built together to become a dwelling in which God lives by his Spirit. (Ephesians 2:19-22)

And, as this passage reminds us, there are no longer foreigners and strangers. Gentiles, the far people, are now at one with the Jews, the near people. It's the biggest mystery of all, this *shalom of oneness,* because the Gentile Church has done all it can to ensure the failure of what Jesus himself brought about ... *for he himself is our peace, who has made the two groups one and has destroyed the barrier, the dividing wall of hostility* (Ephesians 2:14). But God's word always finds fulfilment. It's all a matter of timing.

The end-point though, as stated a couple of chapters back, is for the Church to attain the following authority:

His intent was that now, through the church, the manifold wisdom of God should be made known to the rulers and authorities in the heavenly realms, according to his eternal purpose that he accomplished in Christ Jesus our Lord. In him and through faith in him we may approach God with freedom and confidence. (Ephesians 3:10-12)

We must pray for this outcome. In the meantime, let us reflect and marvel.

Completeness, *shalom*. It's what we all strive for. It's a return to the Garden of Delights (Eden), where there is no separation, no struggle. The words of this popular contemporary song convey this:

I can only imagine what it will be like, when I walk by your side.

THE SHALOM OF SHALOMS

> *I can only imagine what my eyes will see, when your face is before me*
> *I can only imagine.*
> *Surrounded by your glory, what will my heart feel?*
> *Will I dance for you, Jesus? Or in awe of you be still?*
> *Will I stand in your presence? Or to my knees will I fall?*
> *Will I sing hallelujah? Will I be able to speak at all?*
> *I can only imagine. I can only imagine.*
> (*I can only Imagine* by Bart Millard)

Until that day comes, we will continue to put up with wasps, persecution, quiche, late trains, irritations, pesky cats, illness, trauma and misdemeanour in a world of *ra* (do you remember this word, the opposite of shalom). But He gives us a touch of heaven in this world, for those who accept His invitation. He gives the *shalom of salvation*, the greatest shalom available to us, the completeness of being reconciled with our Maker. Then, once we are in God's family, we should be concerned with the *shalom of unity*, finding our place in this wonderful endeavour, whether we have a local, national or even global purpose. Finally, a task for the Church as a whole, an unfulfilled task, but one that has the importance of being a Biblical imperative, the *shalom of oneness*.

There is another way of visualising this, if we consider God's temple in Jerusalem. At the time of Jesus it was comprised of a series of courts. On the outside was the Court of the Gentiles, separated from the rest by a wall. Within this wall was the Court of Women, separated from the Court of Israel by a wall. Within this was a wall separating it from the Court of Priests which, in turn, was separated from the Holy Place and, finally, the Most Holy Place. This hierarchy of courts reflected a hierarchy of privilege. Gentiles stayed on the outside, then Jewish women were allowed to venture a little further and ordinary Jewish men further still. But Priests could go further, right into the Holy Place, but only the High Priest could venture into the Most Holy Place and, even then, only once a year on the Day of Atonement.

When Jesus died on the cross we read the following:

At that moment the curtain of the temple was torn in two from top to bottom. (Matthew 27:51)

The separation between the Holy Place and the Most Holy place was no more. The physical Temple had reached its fulfilment and, from that point onwards, is redefined spiritually.

Don't you know that you yourselves are God's temple and that God's Spirit dwells in your midst? (1 Corinthians 3:16)

This temple has no barriers and, if we remember our Ephesians 2 passage, *the dividing wall of hostility* (vs. 14), the wall that separated the Court of the Gentiles from the rest, is no more and all courts are as one, with even Gentiles now able to enter the Most Holy Place, to access God Himself through prayer. Imagine trying to explain this to a Jew before the time of Jesus, that this whole system, with its hierarchies, rules and restrictions was to collapse into nothing and that everyone – including the Gentiles – would, in future, have the temple living within them! Mind-boggling! This is surely *true Shalom*, but the Church still hasn't really got it.

We need a truly balanced Church, of the far off and the near people, of Gentile and Jew. We need the Jew to find a welcome home without prejudice and we need the Gentile to commit to making a fresh start, unburdened by a frightful history. It's a worthy enterprise and some have already made a start to it. We believe we did so at Foundations 10, though it was more a case of God orchestrating events rather than anything we consciously did ourselves. We are open for a 'repeat performance' at

Foundations 11: One New Man in Derbyshire, where this book will be launched. All is in the Hands of our Wonderful God. But we need to see *One New Man* through to the end. Whether the ideas in this book can play a part in oiling a few gears, then so be it, only God knows this. However it happens, I get a feeling that it *needs to happen*, on a level that we may not currently be able to conceive. Perhaps we are over-involved with thoughts of the *present* – our day to day living as God's ambassadors in an indifferent world – or of the *future* – with the 'blessed hope' sometimes expressed as a *'I'm a Christian, Get me out of here!'* attitude. Maybe *One New Man* is more important than we think?

This mystery is that through the gospel the Gentiles are heirs together with Israel, members together of one body, and sharers together in the promise in Christ Jesus. (Ephesians 3:6)

Think about these words, 'together' (mentioned three times) and 'one body' and ask yourself if the Church is living in this mystery? There is currently very little 'together' with regards to Jews and Gentiles in the Church, so we are living in *ra*, in this respect. The only way we can be in shalom is to work *together* towards a solution. And the onus is with the Gentile Church. Here is some reinforcement, with Paul's exhortations to the Gentile Church:

Consequently, you are no longer foreigners and strangers, but fellow citizens with God's people and also members of his household, built on the foundation of the apostles and prophets, with Christ Jesus himself as the chief cornerstone. In him the whole building is joined together and rises to become a holy temple in the Lord. And in him you too are being built together to become a dwelling in which God lives by his Spirit. (Ephesians 2:19-22)

A House fit for all is what's required, with the wall of partition broken down. Let's get to work through our prayers, attitudes and actions!

FURTHER READING

Now why don't you … ?

At the current time twenty two of Steve's books are available for purchase, either through Christian bookshops or directly from www.sppublishing.com

Into the Lion's Den
Reaching a world gone mad

Daniel was tested in the lions' den. Today, Christians must venture into a very different lion's den and wake up to what is probably the greatest current threat to our witness to the World.

Noise
A search for sense

Noise is everywhere, invading all of our five senses. This incisive, surprising and entertaining book cuts through to the heart of the issue. Is there meaning in the mayhem that has become our World?

To Life!
Rediscovering Biblical Church

Have you ever asked the question, where does the World end and the Church begin? Is the 21st Century Church truly the best it could possibly be?

How the Church lost The Way...
... and how it can find it again

The story of how the Church has been infiltrated by a pagan virus that has worked its way through every facet of our Christian life and how we can start fighting back.

How the Church lost The Truth...
... and how it can find it again

What has happened to some key battlegrounds of Christian Truth and how it is that the Church has managed to lose so much that had been revealed to it in the Bible.

Jesus, the Man of Many Names
A Fresh Understanding from the dawn of time to the End of Days

A book about Jesus that does offer fresh insights without boasting new revelations. Drawing on sources from the Jewish world, ancient and modern, the author will take you on an exhilarating, lively and entertaining exploration of the life and times of the Jewish Messiah.

The Truth is out there
The Ultimate World Conspiracy. Who really is pulling the strings?

Is history just a random sequence of events, or are there secret manipulations? What makes us tick? How did the World as we see it come to be? Read this book if you are prepared to be challenged.

The (other) F-Word
Faith, the Last Taboo

A presentation of the Gospel for the modern world. It is direct, uncompromising, engaging and is written to be relevant to the everyday person. Dare you go where modern man fears to tread? You'll either be inspired or provoked, either way it should be an interesting experience.

Outcast Nation
Israel, The Jews ... and You

The story of the People and the Land through biblical and secular history, tracing the outworkings of God's covenants and offering explanations for both the survival and the success of this Outcast Nation.

God's Signature
The Wonders of the Hebrew Scriptures

Have you ever wondered how the Old Testament came to be written, why God chose Hebrew as the language of the Book and what exactly could we be missing through not reading the Hebrew Scriptures in their original language?**The Bishop's New Clothes**

Has the Church Sold out to the World?

Is the Church as it should be or has it sold out to the World? Is the Body of Christ doing all it could as God's ambassadors or is there room for not so much an improvement as a complete overhaul? This book pulls no punches, but it does so engagingly, with wit and warmth.

God's Blueprint
What does the Old Testament really say?

You will discover recurring themes that build up a wonderful picture of God, the actions and teachings of the Biblical prophets in context, the benefits of viewing the Scriptures Hebraically and new insights revealed by the One New Man Bible translation.

God's Tapestry
What do we do with the Hebrew Scriptures?

This book scratches where most of the Church is itching and cuts right to the heart of some of the controversies concerning how we should be reading and acting on God's Word today.

Hebraic Church
Thinking Differently

Hebraic Church? Now there's a phrase designed to upset or confuse just about everyone. Yet being Hebraic is not what many in the Church imagines it to be. In fact it could be nothing less than the key for true restoration and revival.

Hope
Is there any hope in the World?

Here is a book written to stir the heart of the average citizen of today's world by challenging them to think beyond the here and now. It pulls no punches as it provides a creeping crescendo of revelation regarding man and his relationship with God and how the Church has mostly failed in its mission to mirror the image of Jesus.

Livin' the Life
Christianity rediscovered

Using tools developed over the last few years, the author re-examines a wide spectrum of what we think and how we act as followers of Jesus Christ. To move forwards in our faith we really need to go back to the very beginning.

FURTHER READING

Zionion
Why does the World obsess over Israel?

What's with the British government, the Palestinians, the United Nations, the media, activists, academics, boycotters, some Jews (!), Jihadists, some Christians, neo-Nazis and conspiracy buffs?

The Easter Telling
Easter explained in a Passover service

In this small booklet you have all that you need to re-create this service, primarily following the script indicated in the Gospel accounts, but always in the context of the events of the Exodus, the backdrop of the Passover celebration.

Water
The Stuff of Life

This small book takes you on a fascinating journey into the world of water. From a brief analysis of its structure and unique properties, we look at its function in our bodies and then wonder how it gets to us, through natural means and human ingenuity. We also see its significance in world religions but also see its darker side.

Blood
The River of Life

When it comes to connections, nothing does it better than blood. Silently and unseen it performs its tasks within our body. But it doesn't stop there, blood is identified with other functions that stretch into community, heritage and even further into very surprising places.

Bread

The Food of Life

This small book explores the world of bread. From its origins and history, we look at how it has been made and see it as a metaphor of how our world has gained a degree of complexity, yet has failed in feeding everyone.